Contents

About the Author

Debby DuBay is a Vietnam and Desert Storm Era Veteran, who upon her retirement from the United States Air Force, turned her passion for porcelain into her second profession. Debby DuBay is the owner of Limoges Antiques Shop (www.limogesantiques.com) in downtown Andover, Mass. Ms. DuBay's life has been featured in two best selling books: *The Business of Bliss: How to Profit From Doing What You Love* featured on *Oprah*, and *Turning Your Passion into Profits*. Considered an expert in European and American porcelains, and specializing in Limoges, Ms. DuBay is a Uniform Standards of Professional Appraisal Practices (USPAP) appraiser, a member of the prestigious Appraisers Association of America with an undergraduate degree in psychology, and an MBA. She is a member of the New England Appraisers Association, the Antique Dealers and Collectors National Association, and the Haviland International Club. Ms. DuBay contributes to porcelain books such as *Limoges Boxes* by Faye Strumpf, *The Encyclopedia of Limoges* by Mary Frank Gaston, and Antique Trader's *Antiques & Collectibles, Pottery & Porcelain Ceramics*, and *Teapots* price guides. Ms. DuBay has authored four books on Limoges: *Living With Limoges, Antique Limoges at Home, Collecting Hand Painted Limoges Porcelain—Boxes to Vases* and the *Antique Trader Limoges Price Guide*.

Foreword

For several years, it has been my great pleasure to work with Debby DuBay, whose expansive knowledge of Limoges porcelain has been a tremendous asset in compiling various *Antique Trader* price guides. I'm very pleased to know that she now has the opportunity to focus on her special love in this comprehensive guide.

Limoges is a magical word for those who love beautiful French porcelain. The word is synonymous with fine porcelain but, as you will learn here, the name belongs to a special city in central France. Here, in the 18th and 19th centuries, a number of porcelain factories were established because deposits of the special clays required to produce true hard paste porcelain were located nearby. The best known of these Limoges factories were founded by the Haviland family; however, there were many other firms that produced wares just as fine. Because of the direct marketing of its tablewares to the United States, Haviland has become the most familiar French porcelain here. But all Limoges-made porcelain is high quality and worthy of collector attention.

Another interesting aspect of Limoges is that, by the late 19th century, tremendous quantities of undecorated blanks were exported to the U.S. These plain white pieces then became canvases for amateur china painters. The china-painting hobby was widely popular from the 1880s to about 1920, and thousands of these decorated pieces now find their way to the antiques marketplace.

As you will see by studying this new guide, Limoges porcelain is a vast and fascinating collecting field, offering the collector the opportunity to purchase pretty, but reasonably priced pieces, or extremely fine museum quality rarities. Debby DuBay explains and illustrates all the wonders of Limoges in this great reference.

I know a wonderful treat awaits you in the following pages. Not only is Debby DuBay a true American military hero, but she has also become a dedicated researcher, scholar, dealer, and leading expert in the beautiful world of Limoges porcelain! The following work is a real tribute to her many talents.

Kyle Husfloen, Editor
Antique Trader Books
Editor-at-Large, *Antique Trader Weekly*

Introduction

Antique Trader Limoges Price Guide is my first book in the style of a true collector price guide. After writing my trilogy on collecting Limoges, I did not think there would be a need for any other documentation of the subject, but I was wrong. True collectors can never have enough Limoges, nor can they ever have enough reference books on the subject they are passionate about! A dealer in the field always has a question that requires an immediate answer. This price guide provides that answer quickly. What has been missing for the Limoges lover is a field price guide, in an easy-to-read format, with color photos, complete descriptions, current values, and a marks section.

I conceived *Antique Trader Limoges Price Guide* after more than 35 years of collecting, 13 years of retail selling of fine porcelain as the owner of Limoges Antiques Shop, receiving thousands of e-mails, and responding to verbal requests. We all know how beautiful and inspiring Limoges is, but when on the road, at auction, or Internet collecting, we need a quick price guide that can validate our emotional response of *having to have* that piece of Limoges!

We usually buy what we love, but once armed with information, our beloved collections can also prove to be a great investment. This price guide includes the history of Limoges, a marks section containing common reproduction marks, and hundreds of color photos. Variations of boxes to vases are covered in alphabetical order. Each photograph is followed by a complete description and a current value ensuring that everyone has the information needed to collect Limoges porcelain.

In the following chapters I have photographed pieces that represent the diversity of Limoges porcelain. I would like to thank all the collectors who allowed me to photograph their collections. A special thank you to my mom and the Roy Barefield family; Johanne and Dr. John Ferguson; Candy Gammal; Debbie Grier and her mother Mrs. Elizabeth "Betty" Becker; Debbie and Sam Streiff; Glen Swartz; Lorraine and John Vickers; Janice and Dr. James Wu; North Main Street Antiques; Dan Seldon, Chris Bouchard, and Sean Cocks of North River Auction Gallery; Sandy Collins, owner of Regency Antiques; and Ellie (and Maggie) Smerlas, who have provided photographs of their collection and all the artist's renditions for the marks section in this book. I would like to thank Paul Kennedy for providing me with this opportunity to become an official member of the *Antique Trader* family and allowing me to provide this handy price guide to the Limoges collector. And finally, a sincere thanks to a fellow veteran and my editor, Dan Brownell.

It is my pleasure—and I am always available—to assist a collector, dealer, auctioneer, appraiser, etc. who needs help identifying a piece of Limoges. But with the information provided in the *Antique Trader Limoges Price Guide*, your knowledge will be as good as any expert. I hope you enjoy this handy price guide!

Debby DuBay, Ret, USAF

Valuation

When providing values for a price guide, I do not make up a value or pull a price out of thin air. A considerable amount of professional judgment, experience, and research is used to determine the value of a piece. The Appraisal Institute of America calls this method of finding value the valuation approach. The most commonly used approach for insurance purposes is the market comparison, or comparative market data approach. This method compares the object with similar objects that have been previously sold. The most common marketplace, as named by the Internal Revenue Service, is the retail gallery marketplace.

There are many factors in determining a value for a piece of Limoges, and when comparing, one has to keep in mind the following questions:

- Does the piece have the same mark(s)?
- Is the work by the same artist?
- Is the artist a French factory listed artist, or an amateur American artist?
- Is the piece signed?
- Is the piece factory decorated using the transfer, decal, or mixtion method(s)?
- Are the dimensions the same?
- Is it the same blank?
- Are the age and condition the same?
- When and where was the piece sold?
- Is the data reliable?

For example, in 2006 at an auction house here in the United States, a Limoges vase sold for $3,500. (Keep in mind that the buyer had to add the buyer's premium, sales tax, and shipping costs.) It was then sold in a retail shop for $7,500. This vase was a well-known blank, approximately 15 inches tall, with small double handles, produced in the early 1900s in the William Guerin factory in Limoges, France. It was exquisitely hand painted with a portrait of a woman. But, this selling price does not mean all vases of that blank, hand painted with the portrait of a woman, have the same value. This vase was a once-in-a-lifetime find, as authenticated by the marks on the bottom, which show it was produced in the William Guerin Limoges factory in France. The blank was then exported to the Dresden factory in Germany, where a factory artist exquisitely hand painted it. This piece is the perfect example that all factors must be taken into consideration before assigning a value. It is also an example that the educated collector can still find some valuable pieces of Limoges art on the market today, below its actual value!

Chapter 1

The History of Limoges

Limoges! Whether the name makes you think of a region in France, the city of Limoges, or the factories that produce fine hard-paste Limoges porcelain (in the form of hand-painted decorative pieces of art, dinnerware, or boxes), a picture of romance, beauty, and fabulous artisans probably springs to mind. Historically, the origins of porcelain can be traced to the ancient Orient where Chinese terrain yielded kaolin, a pure white clay that is the essential ingredient in Limoges and other fine hard-paste porcelain. Over 1,000 years ago, the Chinese and Japanese mastered the science of affixing embellishments to glazed porcelain by firing the wares under intense temperatures. During the Age of Enlightenment, Dutch traders imported Chinese porcelain to Europeans eager to forgo domestic earthenware for this delicate, hand-decorated porcelain that appeared translucent when held near the light. The demand for this fine porcelain became so great that the Europeans were determined to duplicate it.

In Germany in 1708, Johann Friedrich Bottger, a chemist under the supervision of the King of Saxony, discovered the formula for producing hard-paste porcelain, while porcelain producers in England, Italy, and France had to settle for bone china or soft-paste porcelain. The newly found formula was well guarded for the next 60 years. Word finally leaked as workers left the German factory and took the formula for the process with them. With the formula now known, and in 1768 the natural essential ingredients of kaolin and feldspar found in the surrounding Limoges region, the porcelain industry was forever changed.

The first porcelain factory in France began production in 1771 in the Limousin region, about 250 miles southwest of Paris. By the 19th century, there were approximately 32 porcelain production factories and 62 decorating studios. By the 1920s, there were more than 48 factories and over 400 known factory marks identifying pieces of Limoges porcelain, including Tressemann and Vogt (T&V), William Guerin (W.G.&Co.), Jean Pouyat (J.P.L.), and Haviland. Limoges has ultimately become the generic name for all of the porcelain produced in the factories in this region. Each factory used a unique factory mark called a backstamp, or under-the-glaze mark. Each piece of Limoges was produced using the same formula of all natural ingredients: feldspar, kaolin, and quartz. And each piece was subjected to an intense firing for 16 hours at about 900 degrees, followed by the glazing process, and yet another firing for eight more hours at approximately 2,000 degrees.

Two factors make a piece of Limoges unique: the shape of the whiteware, or blank, and the process used to decorate it. When the blank was ready, several options were available for decorating it. The blank could be taken to the decorating studio within the factory, sent to another decorating studio within the region, exported to one of the

Example of a plaque hand painted & signed by French factory listed artist "Dubois."

Sample of French factory listed artist signature "E. Furlaud" over master artist signature "D'Apres Gerard."

Sample of French factory listed artist signature "Rancon."

professional decorating factories in the United States, or shipped to department stores or china painting schools for an amateur artist of the era to purchase and hand paint.

Some of the most desired pieces of Limoges are those that were factory decorated and signed by a French factory artist. These pieces would have an underglaze factory mark and an overglaze decorating studio mark and may have the artist's signatures in plain view. Each artist's signature is unique and each artist specialized in a specific subject matter. Some artists were more talented than others. For example, a piece hand painted by Luc is usually far less detailed than a piece hand painted by Dubois. An unusual blank or a complete set hand painted and signed by a talented and desired artist has proven to be an excellent investment today.

Far more common is the factory decorating process known as *decalcomania*, which is a process more commonly known as a decal or transferware. This is the process in which an engraved transfer, like a decal, was placed under the glaze and then fired. Also, many pieces were decorated using the transferware process but then enhanced by a factory artist who hand painted and filled in some of the transferred decoration. Additionally, many pieces with transfer decoration were embellished with hand painted gold details on the rims, edges, handles, and feet. This form of decoration is correctly called *mixtion*. The transferware and mixtion processes made the decoration more durable and were used mainly on dinnerware sets and pieces such as platters, serving pieces, compotes, etc., that were used in some part of the dining ritual.

Most collectors in the United States associate Limoges with the Haviland factories and the very familiar Haviland dinnerware sets that many of us were lucky enough to inherit or have passed down in our families. Due to the strict decorating standards Theodore Haviland set, most dinnerware sets that the Haviland factory produced were also decorated in one of its studios. This fact can be easily verified by looking at the marks on the back of a piece of Haviland. A piece of Haviland dinnerware will have an underglaze factory mark and an overglaze factory decorating mark. By conducting the proper research, a determined collector or appraiser can identify the patterns—not an easy task—as thousands of patterns were used to decorate dinnerware.

Approximately 18,000 barrels of Limoges porcelain were exported to the United States from the late 19th century well into the 20th century. The vast numbers of dinnerware sets, along with the fact that these pieces are not microwave or dishwasher safe, and that our society no longer has sit down dinners for eight to 12 people, has set the price of most dinnerware at an all-time low. Of course there is always the exception; a *complete* set of cobalt blue dinnerware, if found, runs well into the thousands of dollars.

Sample of French factory listed artist signature "Magne."

From the late 1800s to the early 1930s, thousands of blank Limoges pieces were imported to the United States. These blanks were then decorated either at one of the professional American decorating studios—by an artist in one of the many art studios, clubs, and affiliations all across America—or by a wealthy amateur American artist in her home. In 1912, in Chicago alone, there were 49 known decorating studios, and by 1916 that number increased to 102. In addition, decorating studios were operating in New York City, Boston, Philadelphia, Cincinnati, Milwaukee, and Detroit.

Some of the professional decorating studios found in the Chicago area were American Hand Painted China Co.; Burley & Co.; Ceramic Artcraft Studios; Delux China Studios; Edward Donath Studio; France Studios; Illinois China Decorating Co.; Kalita Studio; Keates Art Studio; J.R. Kittler Studio; C.F. Koenig Studios; LeRoy Art Studios; Luken Art Studio; Marmorstein's Art Studio; Osborne Art Studio; Pickard Studios; Pitkin & Brooks; Progressive China Decorating Company; Rivir Studios Inc.; Rogers China Company; Rogers-Martini China Company; E.D. Rogers Co.; Roosevelt China Studio; J.H. Stouffer Company; Tolpin Studios; Tolpin Art Studio; Western Decorating Works; White & White; White's Art Co.; Wright Art Studio; and Yeschek Inc.

Example of a pair of salt & pepper shakers produced (as authenticated by the green underglaze factory mark) & decorated (as authenticated by the red overglaze decorating mark) in the Haviland factory. This pattern name has been identified as the Montmery pattern, as stated on the bottom.

Other companies or groups that decorated blanks imported from Europe were the American Hand Painted China Company; Julius H. Brauer Studio; Claremore Art Studio; Dominick Campana Studio; D.M. Campana Art Company; A. Heidrich Studios; Humboldt Art Studio;

Example of one of the Pickard American professional decorating studio marks.

Example of a signature of listed Pickard artist "McElinels."

Example of a smaller American decorating studio in Chicago, Ill., "Van's China Studio."

International Art Studios; Kay Bee China Works; Parsche Studios; Seidel Studio; and the Pairpoint Studio, New Bedford, Mass. There were also many smaller American decorating studios such as the M. A. Bradford Studio, Boston, Mass.; the New England China Painting Shop, Boston, Mass.; and Van's China Studio, Chicago, Ill. Most of these American studios identified themselves with an overglaze decorating mark on the bottom of the piece of porcelain and are responsible for decorating thousands of blank porcelain pieces imported to the United States from Europe.

Many artists employed in American decorating studios had previously worked in a European porcelain factory before immigrating to the United States. It was also common for an American factory artist to work in several factories over a lifetime, thus creating multiple studio affiliations. Following are names of well-known artists who commercially decorated porcelain in America: Arno, Aulich, Bardos, Beitier, Bentley, Beulet, Beutlich, Blaha, Bohman, Bomyn, Breidel, Burton, Buschbec, Challinor, Cirnacty, Corey, Coufall, Cumming, Donath, Ellsworth, Falatek, Farrington, Fischer, Gasper, Geoss, Gibson, Gifford, Griffiths, Hartman, Heap, Heinz, Hessler, Hiecke, James, Jelinek, Keates, Kiefus, Klipphahn, Koenig, Koep, Leach, Leon, LeRoy, Lindner, Loba, Loh, Marker, McElinels, Miche, Michel, Miller, Motzfeldt, Nessey, Nichols, Nitcshe, Nittel, Passony, Petit, Pfiefer, Pickard, Phol, Pietrykaski, Podlaha, Post, Rawlins, Ray, Rean, Reury, Rhodes, Richter, Roden, Roessler, Ross, Rost, Roy, Samuelson, Schoenig, Schoner, Seagren, Seidel, Shoner, Simon, Sinclair, Stahl, Steiner, Steininger, Thonander, Tolley, Tolpin, Tomascheko, Unger, Vetter, Vobornik, Vokral, Wagner, Walters, Weiss, Weissflog, Wight, Yeschek, and Ziologe.

Limoges production peaked in the Victorian Era (1850-1900), which was named for Queen Victoria's reign (1837-1901). During this period, ostentation and embellishment were commonplace. Obsessed with the rose, Victorians used Limoges blanks as a means of combining their passion for china painting with their love of the flower. By the mid-19th century, one of America's most popular pastimes was china painting. Many American china painters visited Europe to learn the art of china painting, and by the beginning of the 20th century, in the United States alone, more than 25,000 talented artists were enjoying this pastime. The large number of amateur artists accounts for the wide variation in decoration among hand painted Limoges pieces.

The American Artist

Women made huge contributions to the art of painting on porcelain, or china painting. The majority of American china painters were those upper-class women who were allowed creative occupations and those who considered it as a hobby. What developed was a massive cottage industry of women artists who were not only passionate about painting but were extremely skilled and talented. Due to the social mores of the era, these women were never allowed to achieve professional status and were considered amateur artists. (For further information on the impact the female American artist had on china painting, refer to *Collecting Hand Painted Limoges Porcelain—Boxes to Vases.*)

After learning the art of china painting, the amateur artists could purchase the imported blank pieces of Limoges porcelain at fine department stores and studios. Amateur artists did not discriminate against any of the Limoges factories producing these blanks; each artist chose and purchased blanks based on individual interest. Blanks may have been chosen, for example, to fit into a dresser set that an artist was putting together. As a result, most dresser sets have a different factory mark on each piece, although hand painted by the same artist.

Thousands of unknown female artists are responsible for the hand painted pieces of Limoges that most American collectors proudly display today. These pieces are *real Limoges*: fine hard-paste porcelain, produced in the factories in Limoges, France, then imported to the United States as blanks to be decorated by amateur artists or artists in a decorating studio.

Real Limoges is not to be confused with *American Limoges*. American Limoges is not genuine Limoges, but an inferior pottery product produced in the United States. Pottery factories in Ohio used name association to sell their product until 1931, when the City of Limoges Chamber of Commerce filed a lawsuit through the United States State Department contesting the use of the name Limoges. In 1933, by the time the law was enacted, and by 1940 when we see the word "American" added to the mark—the damage was done. Collectors should not confuse a piece of pottery marked American Limoges with French Limoges.

Imported blank pieces of Limoges (also known as whiteware) are marked with an underglaze factory mark (the mark from the factory in Limoges where the piece was produced) on the bottom, literally under the glaze. In addition, someplace on the piece may be the amateur artist's signature, initials, and date. However, many amateur artists did not sign or date their porcelain pieces. There are many fabulous pieces of Limoges art on the market today without a signature. This lack of an amateur artist's signature *does not* affect the value of a piece of hand painted Limoges. Many of these pieces have been handed down from generation to generation, and most of these pieces reach the retail market without any information on the artist. Sad, except that collectors sometimes desire Limoges hand painted by an amateur American artist more than pieces decorated in the Limoges factories. And, although the exact history of the artist may be unknown, the price it commands may be high based on the quality of the painting.

Over the past three decades of researching for my reference resource books on Limoges, I had thought focusing on specific American amateur artists would be of interest to the collector. I became a member of the International Porcelain Artists and Teachers, Inc., (IPAT), an organization that documents porcelain painters, and I visited its museum in Grapevine, Texas. I also contacted porcelain painters and Limoges collectors. I found that collectors generally prefer to collect a consistent subject, such as roses, portrait pieces, cherubs, or game birds, rather than a particular artist. And, because of the lack of family recordkeeping, *unless a painter has become a listed artist,* the amateur American artist is impossible to research.

Ester Miler

This would be the end of this section on the amateur American artist except that I was contacted by a woman in South Carolina, Debbie Grier, who had some questions about her private collection of porcelain hand painted by amateur American artist E. (Ester) Miler. E. Miler's painting on porcelain has become some of the most sought after since her work was featured in 2001 in the book *Living With Limoges* and in 2002 in the book *Antique Limoges at Home.*

According to the United States Federal Census Record, Ester Buckingham Horlbeck was born March 20, 1861, in South Carolina. In the 1880 Census Record, Ester Horlback was living in Charleston, S.C., with her grandmother Mary Seigling, her parents Jonathon and Elizabeth Ottilie Siegling Horlback, and sister Marie B. Horlback. By 1900, the records show Ester married to Edward Barry Miler and residing in the Bronx, New York County, New York State. Mrs. E. Miler had three daughters: Emily O., Ester, and Elizabeth R. She also had a son Edward, who was born and died in 1887. Mrs. E. Miler's middle daughter and namesake Ester died at age 14 on June 22, 1906. In the 1930 Census Record, Mrs. Ester Miler's first name is spelled Est*h*er and it records her and husband Edward Barry Miler living in the town of East Orange, Essex County, New Jersey. This document is the first that lists Mrs. E. Miler's occupation as "artist." On May 29, 1931, at the age of 70, Mrs. E. Miler passed away.

According to tombstone records, Ester Buckingham Horlbeck Miler (20 March 1861-29 May 1931) is buried in the family plot in Magnolia Cemetery, Charleston County, South Carolina. She lies with her husband Edward Barry Miler (who died in 1934), her young daughter Ester, sister Marie Buckingham Horlbeck, and mother Elizabeth Horlbeck.

The Grier story relates the following events: Debbie's mother Mrs. Elizabeth Winifred Troeber Becker, born in 1923, recalls going with her mother Mrs. Mabel Winifred Ott Troeber to Mrs. Miler's home in New Jersey. As a young girl (in an era of frequent entertaining, fine dining, and tea) Elizabeth has fond memories of her visits with her mother to Mrs. Miler's home. She recalls that Mrs. Miler had two rooms full of colorful hand painted china. Mrs. Troeber's aunt— Mrs. Elizabeth Banzer Howell—found Mrs. Miler by word of mouth while living at the Breakers in New York. Mrs. Troeber, Mrs. Howell, and sister-in-law Mrs. Marie Weiss Ott commissioned Mrs. Miler to paint many pieces to include monogramming several dinner sets. Sadly, Mrs. Miler passed away in May 1931 before completing the last commissioned set. The commissioned sets have been handed down to Debbie Grier, a third generation of Miler enthusiasts.

For a time E. Miler used the pseudonym "Hall" and perhaps "Spear's" but research has provided no answers as to why these names were used. If you find a piece of hand painted porcelain signed "Hall," "Miler," or "E. Miler," it is attributed to artist Ester Buckingham Horlbeck Miler. Using pastel colors such as pink and peach and the standard painting technique, she painted roses, apple blossoms, fruits, and berries. Some of her signature pieces have a realistic bumblebee hovering above a flower. Thanks to the story provided by Debbie Grier and her mother Betty, we now have a bit more information on this talented artist, as well as examples of a set of tea and toast plates, a cider pitcher, punch bowl with cups and matching ladle, a squirrel nut dish, and a strawberry tray.

Cabinet displaying the Grier family collection of hand painted Miler.

One of a set of 12 "tea & toasts," consisting of a plate that also acts as a saucer, each cup & plate signed "E. Miler," underglaze T&V factory mark 7 . . . . **Set $1,500**

Cider pitcher, signed "E. Miler," underglaze B&C factory mark 2 . . . . **$600**

Small dish or pin tray, part of dresser set, signed "E. Miler," J.P.L. factory mark 5 . . . . **$100**

Small dish, h.p. w/squirrel, artist signed "E. Miler" (Note: first documentation of an animal h.p. by Miler), underglaze B&C factory mark 2 . . . . . **$300**

Round tray, h.p. w/ strawberries, artist signed "E. Miler," underglaze B&C factory mark 2, 14" d. **$100**

Grier family punch bowl, w/six matching cups, h.p. & signed "E. Miler" inside the bowl near some grapes & near the handles of the cups, underglaze T&V factory mark 5 . . . . **Set $3,500**

Punch cup, artist signed "E. Miler," part of punch bowl set . . . . **Punch Set $3,500**

Ladle, rare, h.p. & signed "E. Miler" in bottom of ladle, part of punch bowl set . . . **Punch Set $3,500**

Teapot & charger, h.p. & signed by "E. Miler" . . . . .teapot **$900** . . . . .charger **$700**

Sample of the signature bee sometimes used by E. (Ester) Miler.

Sample of E. Miler's signature.

Chapter 2

Identifying Limoges Porcelain

The most frequently asked question is if a piece of Limoges *must* be marked. Although most advanced collectors can tell if a piece of porcelain is Limoges by looking at the blank, or shape of the piece of porcelain, I advise collectors to purchase marked pieces of Limoges porcelain. But, there is always the exception. Many pieces of Limoges were not marked if they were produced during the time of the French Revolution. In the 19th century, we find not every piece within a set being marked. We do know that based on the 1891 McKinley Tariff Act, all goods imported to the United States after that date had to list the country of origin *somewhere within the mark*. After 1914, it was also mandatory for all pieces to state "Made In." However, most Limoges factories did not adhere to that requirement until after 1945, especially if their identification mark included the word "Limoges" or "France."

Another frequently asked question relates to pieces that have one of the American Limoges marks. American Limoges is not fine hard-paste porcelain produced in a factory in the Limoges region of France. Rather, it is earthenware produced in the United States from 1897 to 1957, and these factories used name association to entice retail sales of their "Limoges" dinnerware in America during the 20th century. Keep in mind that American Limoges was produced in America for Americans as dinnerware and is *not* fine porcelain nor is it considered fine art.

A piece of Limoges should have a mark or a backstamp under the glaze from the factory that produced that piece of porcelain. This mark is called the whiteware mark, the backstamp, or the underglaze factory mark. This distinct mark identifies which factory in the Limoges region of France produced the piece of porcelain. The mark was placed on the piece prior to being glazed and then fired; thus, the mark is literally under the glaze. This identification mark can be a name, a group of letters, a symbol, or drawing of some sort impressed, stamped, stenciled, printed, or written on the back or bottom of the piece and it is usually green or black in color.

It would be simple to identify a piece of Limoges porcelain produced in the Limoges factories in France if the words "Limoges" or "France" were included in the mark. Very few of the factory marks make identification this easy. With over 400 specific factory marks and the factories in France not adhering to the 1891 McKinley Tariff Act, it is easier to refer to the marks section of this reference book.

There will be a second mark known as the overglaze decorating mark from the studio that decorated the piece. This factory may be the factory that produced the piece

of porcelain or the piece may have been sent to another factory in the region to be decorated. The mark is called the overglaze decorating mark because it is literally on top of the glaze. The overglaze decorating mark is usually much clearer and darker in color than the underglaze factory mark and usually comes in a color other than green, such as red, blue, or purple. Determining if your piece was decorated in the factory is easy: if it has a double backstamp (the underglaze factory identification mark and the overglaze decorating studio mark), it was factory decorated.

Sample of green "T&V Limoges France" underglaze factory mark (also known as the whiteware mark or the backstamp) & "Limoges T&V Hand Painted" red or purple overglaze decorating (or studio) mark.

You may also see a third mark, the French export mark, or the import mark. Import marks are usually easy to identify, as they specifically state the retail department or jewelry store that ordered a piece or a complete set of Limoges to sell in America to the American public. Examples of several retail importers and their import mark: Bailey, Banks and Biddle, Philadelphia; Tiffany's, New York; and Wanamaker's.

A piece of Limoges should have an underglaze factory mark. But, there is always an exception to the rule. Some Limoges plaques were produced and decorated in factories that had their own decorating studio and factory artists. Many times these pieces have only one mark on the back (either the underglaze or overglaze mark), and the factory artist's signature on the front. Also, many of the new (1950s to present) dinnerware sets display their underglaze mark on top of the glaze. This common phenomenon is just a factory mistake. All porcelain imported to the United States since the 1950s absolutely must be marked. If some of the pieces in a dinnerware set make it to the decorating stage without an underglaze factory mark, the mark is applied during the decorating process; thus, the mark is over the glaze.

Sample of green Limoges France underglaze Coiffe factory mark 3, & Flambeau China overglaze mark 4 also in green. Although both marks are green, the underglaze mark is literally under the glaze & the overglaze decorating mark is on top of the glaze. Note the stamp "Hand Painted."

Sample of Elite France over-the-glaze factory export mark in red. This piece of Limoges is being imported to Chas Mayer & Co., Indianapolis (USA).

Chapter 3

Collecting Limoges

Collecting Limoges can be rewarding if one is armed with information. Reproductions pose a serious problem in the market, as hundreds have appeared on the market since the early 1990s. Of course, the quality of their porcelain and artistry is far below the standard of authentic pieces of Limoges produced in the Limoges factories in France. The reproduction pieces are marked with imitation Limoges factory marks and are being sold as Limoges or Limoges China. The most commonly misused marks are T&V (Tressemann & Vogt factory), J.P.L. France (Jean Pouyat factory), Limoges China, and ROC LIMOGES CHINA (ROC standing for Republic of China). A number of factors contribute to the value and desirability of authentic Limoges pieces: the factory where it was produced, mark or marks, age, condition, uniqueness of the blank, size, completeness of a set, and artist's signature. While an amateur artist's signature does not negatively affect value, a French factory listed artist's signature could place a piece of Limoges into investment quality status.

A marked piece of Limoges is a must for a collector, unless it is the exception to the rule or a piece that can be authenticated by matching the blank. An antique piece of Limoges also must be in perfect condition with no repairs. Because Limoges is hard-paste porcelain, it does not craze or crackle like an antique piece of soft-paste porcelain. A piece will be as beautiful and useful as it was when it left the factory in France well over 100 years ago. Hairlines, spiders, cracks, or any damage due to breakage are undesirable and negatively affect the value. Factory and firing imperfections such as pitting and stress fractures around handles are common and do not have a major effect on the value. Paint touch up is undesired, but touching up of gold on handles and trim seems to be a personal preference.

Collecting quality decorative pieces of Limoges can be rewarding and a great investment today, but be sure to collect what you love. There is Limoges available for every taste, and the examples shown throughout this book illustrate the great variety in blanks, decoration, and value.

Reproduction punch bowl.

Inside of reproduction punch bowl. Bowl is marked with the J.P.L. France (Jean Pouyat mark 5).

Reproduction cobalt blue covered box or powder jar.

Common fake mark above the glaze in gold script.

Reproductions

For today's Limoges collector, reproductions are a huge problem. Searching through Internet auction sites, you will find that most pieces are reproductions rather than 19th or 20th century Limoges. All types of pieces are being reproduced, but the most common pieces are vases, tankards, tea and chocolate pots, punch bowls, trays, shoes, and boxes. Many of the reproduced pieces are decorated in cobalt blue, cranberry, and pinks surrounding a transferred scene or floral design, encased in gold.

The following are among the most common fake marks: the fleur-de-lis printed in gold and blue above a banner displaying "Limoges China"; a mark with a crown, above what could be interpreted as crossed swords over the word "Limoges" printed in gold; and the "ROC Limoges" mark, or "ROC Limoges China" mark. The letters "ROC" are an abbreviation for the Republic of China. (Remember that all genuine Limoges is produced in France.) In addition, a large number of reproduction punch bowls have been found with what looks like an authentic J.P.L. France (Jean Pouyat mark 5) on their bottoms under the glaze. By looking closely, you will see that the mark has been fabricated like a sticker, and a heavy shellac-like glaze has been applied over the entire bowl.

See page 267 for reproduction marks.

Tips for Identifying Reproductions

1. Antique Limoges is fine hard-paste porcelain that rings like fine crystal when tapped with a finger. Reproductions make a thud sound.

2. The firing process is what makes Limoges translucent, meaning that light is able to pass through. Reproductions are opaque.

3. The dark blue cobalt color was a difficult color to achieve in the 19th century. Antique pieces of cobalt blue Limoges have a hint of shadowing where the cobalt has run into the porcelain. Reproduction pieces of cobalt blue are very shiny, in perfect condition, and the color has not run.

4. Gold was applied to antique Limoges during or after the final firing. The gold may show some wear and, over time, the gold will have developed a rich patina. Reproduction Limoges displays offensively bright gold in perfect condition.

5. From the French factory-listed artist to the American amateur artist, hand painted Limoges was considered a form of art expression. Pieces were hand painted, then fired seven to eleven times. Reproduction Limoges pieces are mass-produced and display simple childlike painting in bold, bright colors.

6. A piece of antique Limoges will have a factory mark or backstamp called the underglaze mark placed on the bottom when it was still in bisque form. The glaze was then applied and the piece fired, producing a mark that is literally under the glaze. Reproductions may have a decal on the bottom with a shellac-like coating painted over it. Also, many reproduction pieces only have marks that are above the glaze.

7. Antique Limoges must be marked with one of the authentic underglaze factory marks shown in Chapter 36. Reproductions may be marked with one of the reproduction marks identified on page 267, and some are not marked.

8. Antique Limoges underglaze marks are usually black or dark green in color. Reproduction marks are light blue, gray, or gold and some are in script.

9. If decorated in the factory, antique Limoges has an additional mark called the factory decorating mark, which identifies the studio that decorated the piece. Reproductions have only one mark.

10. Antique Limoges is fine hard-paste porcelain that does not crackle or craze. A piece more than 100 years old will look as perfect as the day it came from the factory. Reproductions are a poorly manufactured thick ceramic and will crackle and craze.

New painting on porcelain, not an authentic piece of antique Limoges porcelain. It has no marks on the back.

Chapter 4

Bowls

There are many types of Limoges bowls, such as fluted bowls, fruit bowls, pitcher and bowls, punch bowls, salad bowls, soup bowls, tureens, vegetable bowls, and waste bowls, each with a specific use. (Punch bowls will be addressed in Chapter 29.) Bowls shown in this section that look like punch bowls, due to their size, are correctly identified as fruit bowls. Master fruit bowls are 10 inches in diameter with matching 6-inch serving bowls. The squatty lower bowls with feet and the bowls with a more curvaceous type of flared base are also intended to hold fruit.

Factory decorated fruit bowl, 12" d., 5-1/2" h., underglaze Elite (Bawo & Dotter) mark 5, overglaze Elite (Bawo & Dotter) mark 9 .... $850

Fruit bowl, 9-1/2" d., 4-1/2" h., h.p. w/lemons, opalescence inside, amateur artist signed "K. F. Quinn," underglaze T&V factory mark 8 .... $350

Fruit bowl, 9-1/2" d., 4-1/2" h., h.p. in factory, underglaze T&V factory mark 8, overglaze T&V decorating mark 16b $950

Covered vegetable bowl, 12" d., 3" h., h.p., underglaze Haviland mark $650

Scalloped edged bowl, 12" d., 2" h., h.p., underglaze J.P.L. mark 5 .... $350

Fruit bowl, 9-1/2" d., 4-1/2" h., transferware, underglaze T&V factory mark 5a, overglaze T&V mark 16 .... $150

Small serving bowl, 6" d., 1/2" h., transferware, underglaze Elite (Bawo & Dotter) mark 5, overglaze Elite (Bawo & Dotter) mark 9 .... $25

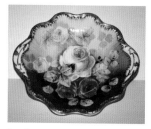

Fruit bowl on base, 9-1/2" d., 4-1/2" h., h.p. & signed by factory artist "Roby," underglaze T&V mark 8, overglaze T&V mark 16 ..... $1,500

Bowl, 12" d., 2" h., h.p. & signed by factory artist "Leona," underglaze Haviland mark & embossed T&H $750

Bowl, 6" d., 4" h., h.p., un-marked **$150**

Serving bowl, 10" d., 3" h., h.p. w/dancing couple, under-glaze Sazerat factory mark 1 . . . . **$475**

Candy bowl, 5-1/2" d., 2" h., h.p. & signed by amateur artist "High," overglaze GDA factory mark 1. . . . . **$175**

Bowl, 12" d., 6" h., h.p., under-glaze factory T&V mark 8. . **$750**

Fruit bowl, 10" d., 3-1/2" h., h.p., underglaze factory Limoges, France, Coiffe mark 2. . . . . **$550**

Bowl, 11" d., 1" h., h.p. & signed by factory artist "Roby," underglaze T&V factory mark 8, overglaze T&V decorating mark 16 . . . .**$450**

Bowl w/gold handles, 18" d., 5" h., h.p., J.P.L., Pouyat factory mark 5. . . . . **$650**

Fruit bowl, 10" d., 4-1/2" h., overglaze J.P.L., Pouyat factory mark 5
. . . . **$1,200**

Bowl, 7" d., 3-1/2" h., h.p. & signed by Pickard artist "Marker," underglaze Guerin factory mark 3. . . . . **$650**

Bowl, 12" d., 4" h., decorated using the mixtion technique, underglaze Lanternier factory mark 4, overglaze Lanternier decorating mark 6. . . . . **$375**

Bowl, condiment or sugar cube bowl, 10" d., 2" h., h.p. & signed by amateur artist "Ida Limpton Paiga," underglaze J.P.L. mark 5 . . . . **$150**

Bowl, small condiment bowl, 10" d., 3" h., h.p. by unknown amateur artist, underglaze T&V mark 7 . . . . **$200**

Nut bowl, 3" d., 2" h., h.p. w/ amateur artist signature "J. A. Barbour," underglaze T&V mark 7. . . . . **$250**

Celery bowl, 11" d., 2" h., h.p. w/portrait & heavy gold gild w/scrollwork, underglaze T&V factory mark 8 . . . . **$350**

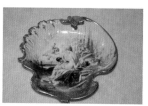

Bowl, small oblong, 3" d., 1-1/2" h., h.p. w/illegible amateur artist initials, underglaze D&C mark 3 . . . . **$150**

Hand painted bowl, 8" d., 2-1/2" h., h.p. w/couple, underglaze J.P.L. factory mark 5 . . . . **$450**

Celery bowl, 11" d., 2" h., h.p. w/roses, underglaze T&V factory mark 8. . . . . **$250**

Pudding bowl w/ under plate, 12" d., 4" h., factory decorated using the mixtion technique of embellishing a transfer, gold gild on rim, plate w/identical decoration & marks, underglaze T&V mark 8, overglaze T&V mark 16. . **Set $350**

Bowl, 8" d., 2" h., h.p. w/grapes, underglaze Lanternier factory mark 4. . . . . **$195**

Bowl, 12" l., h.p. w/cherub & burnished gold gild, underglaze Klingenberg factory mark 7, overglaze Klingenberg decorating mark 9 . . . . **$450**

Bowl, 9-1/2" d., amateur artist signed "A. Burton," underglaze J.P.L. factory mark 5 . . . . **$225**

Centerpiece bowl, 9" d., 3" h., h.p. & signed by factory listed artist "Leon," Theodore Haviland factory mark P **$650**

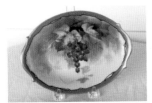

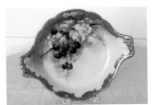

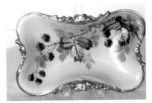

Bowl, 6" d., amateur artist signed "Hammer," underglaze T&V factory mark 7, overglaze Jul H. Brauer mark **$275**

Bowl w/tab handles, 8" d., 6" h., h.p. & artist signed "Lobo," underglaze T&V factory mark 7, overglaze Pickard decorating studio mark **$550**

Rectangle bowl, 8-1/2" d., 5" h., h.p. & artist signed "Steve," underglaze J.P.L. factory mark 5a **$200**

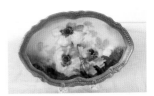

Bowl, 6" d., 4" h., h.p., underglaze Borgfeldt factory mark 1 . . . . **$175**

Master bowl, 10-1/2" d., & four matching bowls, 6" d., h.p. & artist signed "Henrod," underglaze Coiffe factory mark 3 . . . . **Set $450**

Bowl, 9" d., h.p. w/illegible signature, underglaze GDA factory mark 1, overglaze Pickard decorating studio mark **$450**

Chapter 5

Boxes

Limoges boxes have been highly collectible because of their usefulness in holding small precious objects for safekeeping. During the 19th century and Victorian Era, Queen Victoria was known for using Limoges boxes to hold precious and sentimental items such as baby teeth and locks of hair. In the 20th century, Limoges boxes became very collectible and were produced for a variety of items ranging from cigarettes to jewelry. Today thousands of Limoges boxes are on the market, with those produced and hand painted in the factories in France being desirable pieces of miniature art. Several factories are known for their quality boxes: Rochard, Artoria, S&D Limoges, and Chamart.

Cobalt box, enamel, 19th c., marked "Made in France," 3 x 5", 3" h. **$2,000**

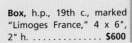

Box, h.p., 19th c., marked "Limoges France," 4 x 6", 2" h. **$600**

Box, mixtion, ca. 1960, Limoges Castel mark, 3" d., 1/2" h. **$400**

Box, h.p., ca. 1960, Limoges Castel mark, 2 x 4-1/2", 4" h. **$400**

Box, ca. 1920, marked "Limoges France," 2" d., 1/2" h. **$450**

Box, h.p., w/raised white enamel, ca. 1920, marked "Limoges France," 2" d., 1/2" h. **$450**

Box, h.p., w/raised enamel scrollwork, ca. 1920, marked "Limoges France," 8" d., 6" h. **$850**

Box, h.p., ca 1950, Limoges Castel mark, 6" d., 3" h. **$600**

Box, heart shaped, h.p., ca. 1960, Limoges Castel mark, 2" d., 1/2" h. **$400**

Box, h.p., ca. 1950, Limoges Castel mark, 3" d., 1" h. **$400**

Box, h.p. gold, transfer cherubs, ca. 1950, Limoges Castel mark, 3" d., 1" h. **$400**

Box, h.p., raised gold paste, artist signed "Paul," ca. 1970s, underglaze Limoges France mark 1, overglaze "Porcelaine de' corr'r la s'main Paris Style" **$400**

Box, heart shaped, h.p., w/raised gold enamel, 19th c., marked "France," 3" d., 2" h. **$700**

Box, cobalt, h.p. by factory artist & signed "Rex" 19th c., marked "France," 11" d., 7" h. **$4,000**

Box, heart shaped, h.p., raised gold paste, artist signed "Lemas," ca. 1970, Limoges Castel mark, 3" d., 1/2" h. **$300**

Box, h.p. w/raised white enamel, ca. 1950, Limoges Castel mark, 3" d., 1" h. **$400**

Box, teapot shape, h.p., ca. 1970, Limoges Castel mark, 3" d. . . .**$200**

Box, h.p., ca. 1970, Limoges Castel mark, 3" d., 1" h. **$200**

Box, h.p. w/flowers & burnished gold, ca. 1940, Limoges Castel mark, 14" d., 6" h. **$4,000**

Box, h.p. w/raised black enamel, ca. 1940, Limoges Castel mark, 3" d., 1" h. **$200**

Box, bisque w/raised cherubs, early 20th c., Limoges France mark 2, 7" d., 5" h. **$500**

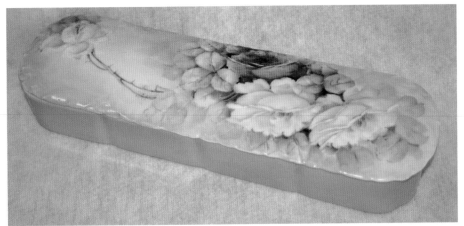

Box, glove box, h.p. by unknown artist, matches hankie box, underglaze D&C mark 3, 2 x 15", 2" h.
.... **$650**

Box, dresser or hankie box, h.p. by unknown artist, underglaze D&C mark 3, 8 x 8", 3" h........ **$650**

Box, dresser box, h.p. by unknown artist w/dark dramatic roses, underglaze D&C mark 3, 2 x 10", 3" h..................... **$650**

Chapter 6

Belt buckle brooch or pendant, oval, h.p. portrait of Queen Louise w/real pearl necklace, sterling silver bezel, 19th c., 3-1/2" d. **$700**

Brooches and Buttons

Some of the most beautiful pieces of Limoges are tiny brooches and hand painted buttons. Portraits were made of famous people such as Queen Louise, Joan of Arc, Madame Pompadour, Marie Antoinette, Napoleon and Josephine, and George and Martha Washington. But there were no rules for the amateur artist, who could paint anything from a beloved pet or a relative to a favorite flower on a brooch or button. It is this diversity, and their relatively reasonable price, that make collecting these fascinating tiny miniatures rewarding and fun.

Belt buckle brooch or pendant, oval, h.p. portrait of Queen Louise in sterling silver bezel, 19th c., 4-1/2" d. **$800**

Belt buckle brooch or pendant, oval, h.p. portrait of Queen Louise in ornate brass-plated bezel, 19th c., 5-1/2" d. **$700**

Belt buckle brooch or pendant, oval, h.p. portrait of Martha Washington, unusual colors & subject matter, in gold braided bezel, 19th c., 3-1/2" d. **$700**

Brooch, oval, decorated w/ European royalty, raised gold paste, 19th c., 2" d. **$200**

Brooch, oval, decorated w/ European royalty, raised white enamel at bodice, 19th c., 2" d. **$200**

Brooch, oval, decorated w/"painted lady," a bit provocative w/plunging neckline, raised white enamel for pearls, 1915-1930s, 1-1/2" d. **$200**

Brooch, oval, decorated w/portrait of woman, h.p. w/raised gold paste, late 19th c. or early 20th c., 1-3/4" d. **$300**

Brooch, heart shaped, decorated w/European lovers, illegible artist's signature, 14k gold twisted bezel, late 19th c. or early 20th c., 2-1/2" d. **$800**

Brooch, heart shaped, decorated w/European lovers, partial h.p. & transfer, 14k gold filled bezel, late 19th c. or early 20th c., 2-3/4" d. **$400**

Brooch, unique shape, h.p., embellished w/raised enameled dots & gold paste, ca. 1900, 1-1/4" d. **$200**

Brooch, round, decorated w/ maiden's portrait, raised gold paste & blue enamel dots, ca. 1900, 7/8" d. **$200**

Brooch, round, decorated w/ Art Nouveau maiden's portrait, raised gold paste, 1890-1915, 7/8" d. **$200**

Brooch, unique clover shaped, decorated w/h.p. forget-me-nots, burnished gold stem, ca. 1900, 1-1/2" d. **$75**

Brooch, watch fob, heart shaped, decorated w/maiden's portrait, partial h.p. & transfer, ca. 1900, 1" d. **$400**

Belt buckle brooch, h.p. roses, thick raised gold-paste border, brass back, early 1900s, 4" d. **$600**

Brooch, elongated, h.p. roses, brass back, early 1900s, 3" d., 4-1/2" l. **$600**

Brooch, can be used as pendant, oval, decorated w/h.p. roses on black enamel, 14k gold back & heavy rope bezel, late 19th c. or early 20th c., 4" d. **$800**

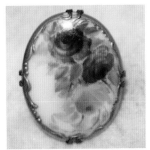

Brooch, oval, decorated w/h.p. roses & raised gold paste, late 19th c. or early 20th c., 1-3/4" d. **$200**

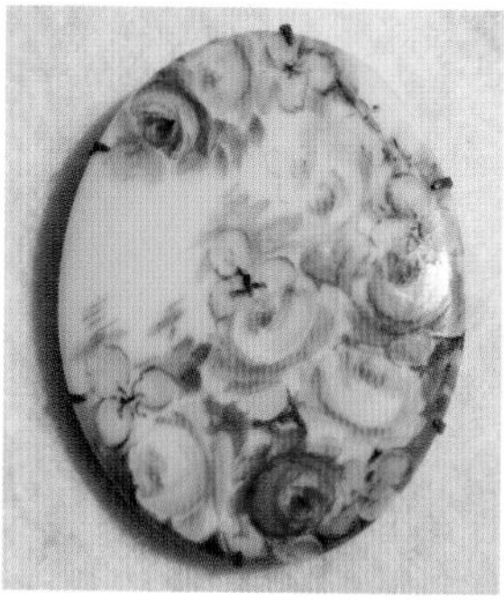

Belt buckle brooch, oval, h.p. roses, brass back, ca. 1900, 3-1/2" d. **$400**

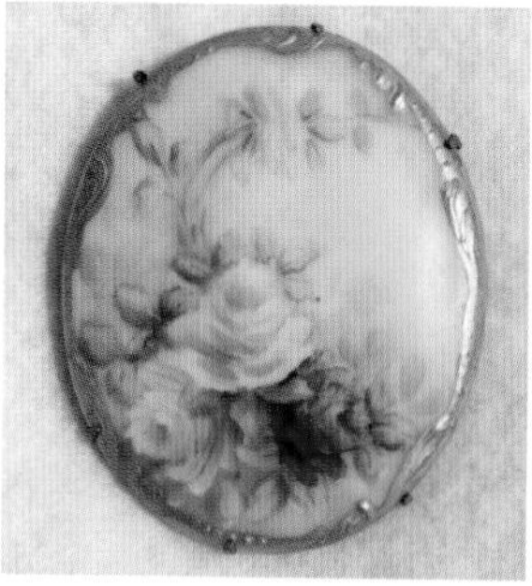

Belt buckle brooch, oval, h.p. roses, thick raised gold paste, brass back, ca. 1900, 3-1/2" d. **$450**

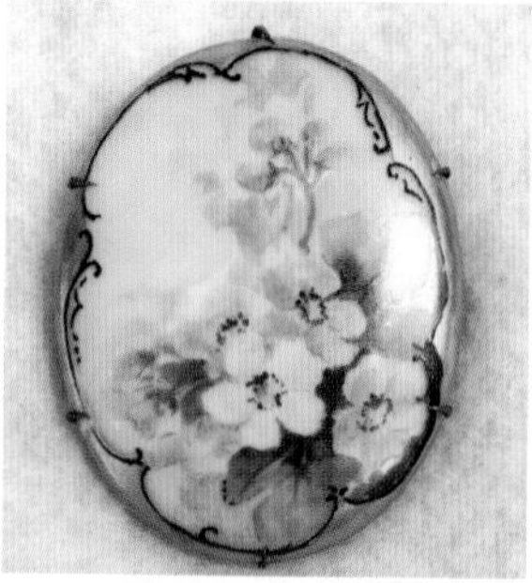

Brooch, oval, h.p. wild roses, irregular burnished gold border outlined in black, brass back, ca. 1900-1917, 2-1/2" d. **$150**

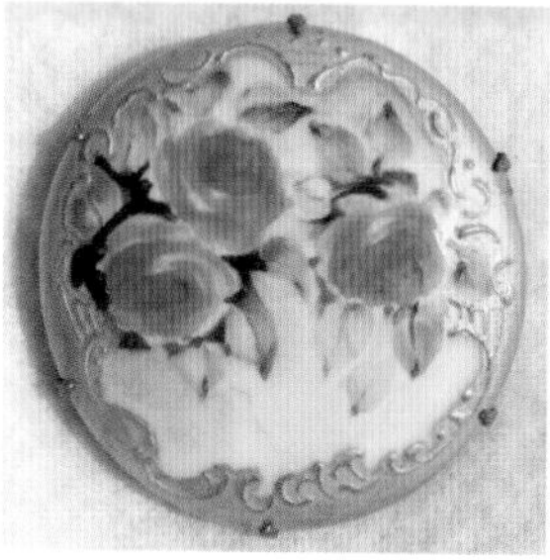

Brooch, round, h.p. dark roses, thick raised gold paste, brass back, ca. 1900, 3-1/2" d. **$450**

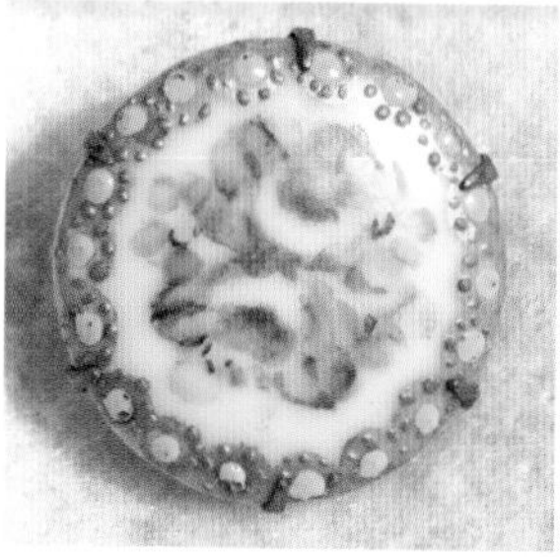

Brooch, round, h.p. roses, thick raised gold paste w/raised blue enamel dots, brass back, ca. 1900, 1-1/2" d. **$150**

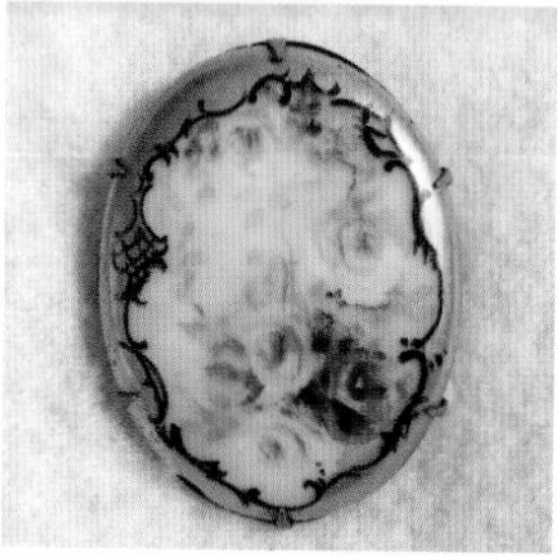

Brooch, oval, h.p. roses, irregular burnished gold border outlined in black, brass back, ca. 1900-1917, 2-1/2" d. **$150**

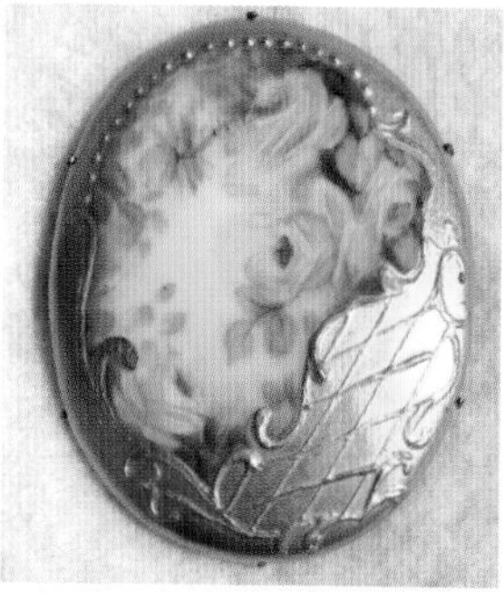

Belt buckle brooch, oval, h.p. roses, thick raised gold paste w/scrolling, brass back, ca. 1900, 3-1/2" d. **$350**

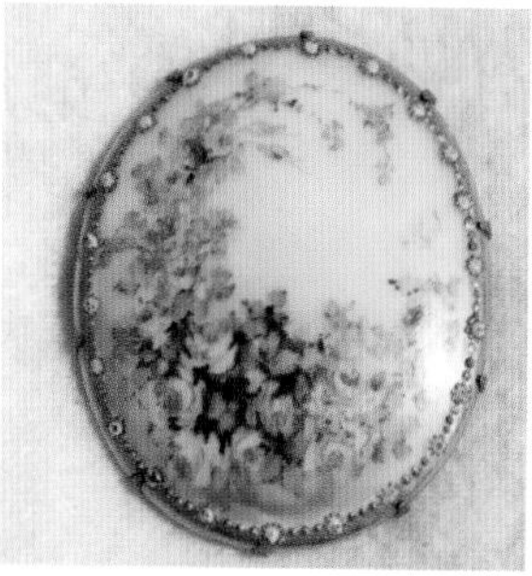

Belt buckle brooch, oval, finely h.p. roses, raised gold-paste border w/raised enamel blue dots, brass back, ca. 1900, 3-1/2" d. **$450**

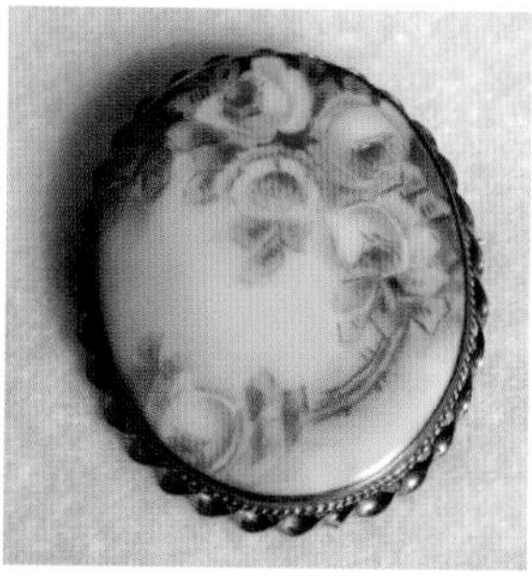

Brooch, oval, decorated w/h.p. roses in standard method of painting, heavy 14k gold back & heavy rope bezel, late 19th c. or early 20th c., 5" d. **$500**

Brooch, oval, decorated w/h.p. roses on white enamel, heavy 14k gold back & heavy rope bezel, late 19th c. or early 20th c., 5" d. $800

Brooch, oval, decorated w/h.p. forget-me-nots, thick raised gold paste, early 20th c., 2" d. . . . $200

Brooch, round collar or sash brooch, w/h.p. lilies (meaning return of happiness), artist's initials "M.H.R.," late 19th c. or early 20th c., 2" d. $250

Brooch, round, decorated w/h.p. forget-me-nots, raised gold paste & blue enamel dots, early 20th c., 2" d. $200

Brooch, round, decorated w/h.p. violets & raised white enamel dots, ca. 1900, 7/8" d.. . . . . . $100

Belt buckle brooch, oval, decorated w/h.p. forget-me-nots, thick raised gold paste w/scrolling, early 20th c., 3-1/2" d. . $400

Brooch, oval, decorated w/h.p. forget-me-nots, ornate & thick raised gold paste, early 20th c., 2" d. $200

Belt buckle brooch, oval, decorated w/h.p. forget-me-nots, early 20th c., 3-1/2" d. $200

Belt buckle brooch, oval, h.p. w/ raised gold paste & blue enamel dots, early 20th c., 2-1/2" d.. **$200**

Brooch, oval collar or sash brooch, w/h.p. violets & raised gold paste, brass back, ca. 1900, 2-1/2" d.
. . . . **$250**

Brooch, round collar or sash brooch, w/h.p. geometric & intricate designs w/thick burnished gold, Exotic Revival period, ca. 1880, 3-1/2" d.
. . . . **$300**

Brooch, round collar or sash brooch, w/h.p. violets (meaning faithfulness & modesty) w/raised scrolled gold paste, ca. 1900, 2-1/2" d.
. . . . **$300**

Brooch, round, decorated w/violets & burnished gold, 1890-1915, 7/8" d. **$100**

Brooch, oval, decorated w/h.p. violets on white enamel, heavy 14k gold back & heavy rope bezel, late 19th c. or early 20th c., 4" d.
. . . . **$600**

Brooch, crescent shaped, decorated w/h.p. water lilies & burnished gold tips, brass embellishments, ca. 1900, 1-1/2" d. **$75**

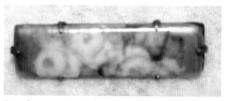

Brooch, rectangular shaped, decorated w/h.p. roses & burnished gold tips, brass embellishments, ca. 1900, 1-1/2" d. **$75**

Bar pin brooch, h.p. w/roses, c. 1900 . . . . **$75**

Bar pin brooch, h.p. w/single elongated daisy (meaning innocence & beauty) & burnished gold, c. 1900
. . . . **$50**

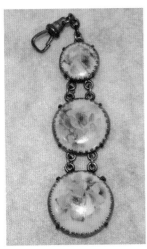

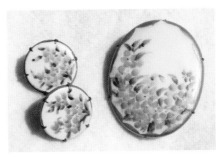

Belt buckle brooch, oval, w/matching earrings, decorated w/h.p. forget-me-nots, early 20th c., 3-1/2" d. . . **Set $200**

Pair of belt buckle brooches, oval, h.p. roses, thick burnished gold, brass back, ca. 1900, 3-1/2" d. . **Pair $750**

Rare lady's watch fob, h.p. w/pink roses & raised gold paste attached together w/chain, back marked "France," ca. 1880, 4-3/4" l. **$350**

Pendant, round, decorated w/h.p. forget-me-nots, raised gold paste & white enamel embellishments, gold filled, ca. 1900, 2" d. . **$200**

Brooch, oval, decorated w/h.p. violets, burnished gold rim, ca. 1900, 1-1/2" d. **$200**

Brooch, oval, decorated w/h.p. violets on white enamel, heavy brass back & frame, ca. 1900, 2-1/2" d. **$300**

Brooch, round, unique four leaf clover design & thick burnished gold, 1890-1915, 2" d. **$150**

Pair of buttons, h.p. w/red, pink & yellow roses, surrounded w/ burnished gold, ca. 1900, 1" d. . . . . **Pair $100**

Pair of buttons, h.p. w/red & pink roses, tiny bit of burnished gold, ca. 1900, 3/4" d. . . . . Pair $50

Set of four buttons, h.p. w/red, pink & white roses, surrounded w/raised gold paste & enamel dots, ca. 1900 . . .Set $200

Pair of studs/buttons, h.p. w/red, pink & white roses, surrounded w/ raised gold paste, ca. 1900, 3/4" d. . . . . Pair $100

Pair of buttons, h.p. w/red & pink roses & burnished gold, ca. 1900, 3/4" d.. . Pair $50

Card of buttons, h.p. w/roses & raised scrolled gold paste, ca. 1900, 3/4" d. . . . . Set $100

Button/stud, h.p. w/red, pink & white roses, surrounded w/thick raised gold paste & raised enamel blue dots in the shape of a heart, 3/4" d. $75

Set of four square buttons/studs, h.p. w/roses outlined in burnished gold, ca. 1900, pair 3/4" d., pair 1/2" d.. . . . . . . .Set $100

Pair of studs/buttons, h.p. w/red & pink roses & greenery, ca. 1900, 1" d. . . . . Pair $150

Set of four round studs, w/ matching oval button, h.p. w/ pink roses outlined in raised gold paste w/enamel blue & white dots, ca. 1900, pair 3/4" d., pair 1/2" d., button 1" d.. . . .Set $250

Set of four round buttons, h.p. w/pink roses outlined in burnished gold & small raised gold enamel dots, ca. 1920, 1" d. .Set $300

Button/stud, h.p. w/forget-me-nots, surrounded w/thick raised gold paste, ca. 1900, 3/4" d. $75

Button/stud, h.p. w/for-get-me-nots & white raised enamel, ca. 1900, 3/4" d. **$25**

Pair of studs/buttons, h.p. w/pansies & burnished gold, ca. 1900, 1" d. . . . .**Pair $150**

Pair of studs/buttons, h.p. w/dark violets & greenery, ca. 1900, 1" d. . . . . **Pair $50**

Pair of studs/buttons & a larger button, h.p. w/pur-ple & blue violets & burnished gold, ca. 1920, 1" d. . . . . **Set $50**

Brooch, oval, decorated w/sil-houette of ship, opalescent back-ground, ca. 1900, 1-3/4" d. . **$100**

Pair of studs/buttons, h.p. w/violets & burnished gold, ca. 1900, 1" d . . . .**Pair $50**

Brooches and Buttons 45

Chapter 7

Cake Plates

Cake plates normally have double handles for serving and are 10 to 13 inches in diameter. Cake plates were sometimes part of a complete dessert set consisting of a cake plate, six to 12 dessert plates, and matching cups and saucers. Most factory dinnerware sets did not include a dessert set, but a dessert set could be ordered separately. Today, dessert sets and cake plates that were decorated in the factory using the transferware method are fairly common and reasonably priced. Dessert sets and cake plates hand painted by the amateur artists of the 19th and 20th centuries could consist of randomly selected blank pieces of Limoges, creating a distinct and unique dessert set. Hand painted sets and cake plates are very desirable and priced accordingly.

Cake plate, 11" d., h.p. by amateur artist, underglaze Gerard, Dufraisseix & Morel mark 2 .... **$450**

Cake plate, 11" d., h.p. & signed by factory artist "Henria," underglaze Coiffe mark 3, overglaze Flambeau decorating mark 4 .... **$450**

Cake plate, 11-1/2" d., h.p. in Pickard factory, Pickard gold mark, underglaze B&C France mark 1 ... **$750**

Cake plate on pedestal, 12" d., h.p., underglaze T&V factory mark 8 .... **$400**

Cake plate, 11" d., transfer, underglaze Limoges France factory mark 1, overglaze Limoges France decorating mark 1 in red
. . . . **$150**

Cake plate, 16" d., h.p. & artist signed "March," underglaze T&V factory mark 8
. . . . **$950**

Cake plate, 11" d., h.p. underglaze Granger factory mark 2. . . . . **$450**

Cake plate, 11-1/2" d., h.p. w/roses & ornate raised gold paste, underglaze Haviland France factory mark 1. . . . . **$350**

Cake plate, 11-1/2" d., h.p., w/artist's initials "A.A.E.," underglaze Haviland France factory mark 1. . . . . **$350**

Cake plate, 11-1/2" d., h.p. w/artist signature "J.J. Driscoll" & dated 1910, underglaze T&V factory mark 8. . . . . **$350**

Cake plate, 11-1/2" d., cranberry w/burnished gold, underglaze & overglaze Limoges Castel mark **$350**

Cake plate, 10-1/2" d., decorated in the factory w/burnished gold, underglaze Bawo & Dotter (Elite) factory mark 5, overglaze decorating Bawo & Dotter decorating mark 9 .... **$250**

Cake, dessert, or truffle plate, 11" d., h.p. w/artist's initials "M.E.H." & dated 1898, impressed whiteware mark "AL" w/underglaze Lanternier factory mark 4. .... **$450**

Cake plate, 11" d., h.p., underglaze Granger factory mark 2 .... **$300**

Cake plate, 9-1/2" d., h.p. cobalt & Vellum painting of flowers & fruit overhanging a lake w/swans, underglaze Limoges Gimbel Bros., factory mark 1, attributed to Pickard. **$750**

Cake plate, 9" d., h.p., underglaze Haviland factory mark C. **$250**

Cake plate, 10" d., h.p., underglaze T&V factory mark 8. .... **$250**

Cake Plates 49

Chapter 8

Chargers

The Limoges charger, or chop plate, as it was called during the 19th century, has become a popular piece of art today. Characteristically, chargers were produced in factories to match a dinnerware set. Once the china painting fad became popular in the United States, amateur artists began using this large round piece of porcelain as a canvas to hand paint and decorate. Chargers are a minimum of 12 inches in diameter with scalloped or embellished edges and are used today as wall art.

Charger, 12" d., decorated in factory using mixtion, artist signature "Gilbot" stamped on front, underglaze Bawo & Dotter (Elite) factory mark 5, overglaze Bawo & Dotter decorating mark 8 . . . . . **$400**

Charger, 14" d., h.p. & signed by amateur artist "Pauline Winslow," underglaze D&C factory mark 3. . . . . **$800**

Charger, 13" d., h.p. & signed by amateur artist "M.P. Heine," underglaze T&V factory mark 8 . . . . **$850**

Charger, 12" d., h.p. w/violets by unknown artist, underglaze Klingenberg factory mark 6 . . . . **$400**

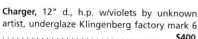

Charger, 16" d., dramatic painting of roses by unknown amateur artist, underglaze T&V factory mark 8 . . . . $1,200

Charger, 17" d., factory h.p. & signed "Duval," heavy burnished gold w/ornate etching, underglaze T&V factory mark 7 . . . . $3,000

Charger, 17" d., factory h.p. & signed "Duval," heavy burnished gold w/ornate etching, underglaze T&V factory mark 7 . . . . $3,000

Chapter 9

Chocolate and Coffee Pots

The French created the chocolate pot, also known as a *chocoliatiere*, in the 17th century. This pot was extremely popular during the Victorian Era when mothers served their children hot chocolate or cocoa as a breakfast or mid-morning beverage and sometimes as a substitute for afternoon tea. The distinguishing characteristic of all pots is the spout. The chocolate pot's spout is close to the top of the pot and is very stubby and short. Chocolate pots are usually tall and narrow and can range in height from 5 inches for a single pot, to 10 inches for a four-cup pot, to 12 inches for a six- to eight-cup pot. The lid of the pot may have a factory-placed hole for a long silver spoon to be inserted to stir the chocolate that may have settled on the bottom.

Americans love coffee, and because one would never use a chocolate or teapot to serve coffee, a demand was created for a specific pot. The coffee pot has a spout that is closer to the base of the pot and is much straighter than that of a teapot and longer than that of a chocolate pot. A coffeepot is designed to be 7 to 13 inches tall to allow coffee grounds to sink to the bottom. Confusion as to whether a pot is a teapot or coffee pot occurs because iced tea was sometimes served in coffee pots. Further confusion comes from 19th century china catalogs that featured both tea and coffee pots. Due to the popularity of iced tea, many coffee sets were advertised as "pots large enough to hold iced tea." When trying to determine the original use of a pot, keep in mind that the spout is the distinguishing feature.

Chocolate set: tray, tea & chocolate pot, 6 cups & saucers, matching cake plate; J.P.L. factory mark 5. . . . . **Set $1,000**

Chocolate set: pot, six cups & saucers & tray; factory h.p. & artist signed "Magne," underglaze T&V factory mark 7, overglaze T&V decorating mark 11 . . .**Set $3,000**

Chocolate set: pot, eight cups & saucers, eight dessert plates & cake plate; factory h.p. & artist signed "Henria," underglaze Coiffe factory mark 3, overglaze Flambeau China decorating mark 4 . . . .**Set $3,500**

Chocolate set: pot, six cups & saucers, tray, h.p. by unknown amateur artist who picked blank pieces from different factories to paint; pot: underglaze GDA factory mark 1; tray: T&V factory mark 8; cups & saucers: J.P.L. factory mark 5. . . . . **Set $2,000**

Chocolate set: pot, six cups & saucers, tray, h.p. by unknown amateur artist, underglaze J.P.L. factory mark 5 . . . . **Set $3,000**

Chocolate set: pot, four cups & saucers, four dessert plates, factory decorated using transferware/decal method, underglaze J.P.L. factory mark 5, overglaze J.P.L. decorating studio mark 9 . . . . . **Set $350**

Coffee set: pot, sugar & creamer w/four cups & saucers, embellished gold w/decal, underglaze Plainemaison factory mark 1 . . . . **Set $700**

Chocolate set: pot, four cups & saucers, tray; h.p. by unknown amateur artist who selected blank pieces from different factories to paint; pot: marked Bavaria; tray: T&V factory mark 8; cups & saucers: J.P.L. factory mark 5 . . . . **Set $1,000**

Chocolate set: pot, six cups & saucers, dessert plates, cake plate & teapot, h.p. by unknown amateur artist who selected blank pieces from different factories to paint; chocolate pot: J.P.L. factory mark 5; cake plate: J.P.L. factory mark 5; rest of set (teapot, creamer, sugar, cups, saucers, & dessert plates) marked Bavaria . . . . **Set $1,000**

Chocolate set w/four cups&saucers,creamer & sugar, Haviland Cie factory mark H . . . .**Set $2,000**

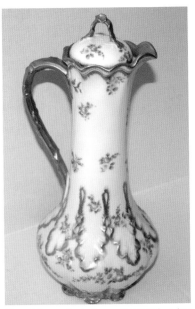

Chocolate pot, factory decorated using transferware/decal method; underglaze GDA factory mark 1, overglaze GDA decorating mark 4. . . . . **$150**

Chocolate pot w/four cups & saucers, underglaze Pouyat factory mark 5 . . . . **Set $900**

Chocolate pot, h.p. w/blackberries, underglaze J.P.L. mark 5 . . . . **$500**

Coffee pot (placement of spout differentiates a chocolate pot from a coffee pot), cobalt blue, underglaze & overglaze Limoges France mark 6 . . . . **$500**

Chapter 10

Cider Pitchers

Cider pitchers were used to serve cider, juices, and sometimes lemonade. They are differentiated from a tankard by their use, squatty shape, substantial handles, and short height of 5 to 6 inches. Cider pitcher sets include the matching mugs and tray, although most mugs have not survived.

Cider set: pitcher 10" h., 12" d., mugs 4" h., tray 18" d., h.p. by amateur American artist E. Miler (see pgs. 14-15 in the American Artist section of Chapter 1), underglaze WG&Co. factory mark 3
.... **Set $3,000**

Cider set: pitcher 10" h., 12" d., mugs 4" h., tray 16" d., h.p. by amateur American artist, etching using burnish gold, underglaze J.P.L. factory mark 5 ....**Set $600**

Cider pitcher, 9-1/2" h., 10-1/2" d., factory h.p. & artist signed "Roby," underglaze T&V factory mark 5a, overglaze T&V decorating mark 15 . . . . . $1,500

Cider pitcher, 8-1/2" h., 9" d., h.p. & signed by amateur artist "Worth," underglaze Haviland France factory mark 1 . . . . $1,000

Cider pitcher, 5" h., 9" d., h.p. & signed by amateur artist "B. Young Shook," underglaze J.P.L. factory mark 5. . . . . $650

Cider pitcher, 5" h., 9" d., h.p. by unknown amateur artist, underglaze J.P.L. factory mark 5. . . . . . . $550

Cider pitcher, 6" h., 8" d., h.p. & signed by amateur artist "F H Robinson," J.P.L. underglaze factory mark 1 . . . . $550

Cider pitcher, 3" h., 4-1/2" d., h.p. by unknown artist w/no identification marks $100

Cider pitcher w/tray, pitcher 5" h., 9" d., tray 16" d., h.p. by amateur artist, underglaze J.P.L. factory mark 5 . . . . **Set $850**

Cider pitcher, 6" h., 8" d., h.p. & signed "Colon," underglaze J.P.L., Pouyat factory mark 5 . . . . **$550**

Cider pitcher, 6-1/2" h., 9" d., h.p. in White's Decorating Studio USA, underglaze W.G.&Co., factory mark 2, overglaze White's Art Co., Chicago, in red **$800**

Cider pitcher, 6-1/2" h., 9" d., h.p. in Pickard factory, artist signed "E. Challinor," underglaze factory mark W.G.&Co., overglaze "Hand Painted Pickard China" factory mark . . . **$1,500**

Pitcher w/scroll design base, 10" h., h.p., underglaze GDA factory mark 1 . . . . **$350**

Cider pitcher, 9" h., h.p. w/plums, underglaze GDA factory mark 1 . . . . **$450**

Pitcher, 9" h., h.p. w/cherries, underglaze GDA factory mark 1 . . . . **$200**

Pitcher, 9" h., h.p. w/blackberries, Haviland mark 11 . . . . **$550**

Pitcher, 10" h., h.p. w/blackberries, GDA factory mark 1. . . . . **$550**

Chapter 11

Clocks

Limoges factories produced and decorated beautiful clock cases designed to hold Swiss movements. Mantel clocks with matching candelabra, smaller ladies clocks, and hanging clocks were also produced, factory decorated, and exported.

Hanging wall clock, bronze chain, handles & top surround porcelain case, h.p. w/raised enamel blue & white flowers, marked "France," ca. 1860s, 14" d. **$3,500**

Travel clock, unique top opens to display clock, ca. 1930s, 11" h. **$600**

Mantel clock, ornate w/cherub scene, artist signed "Quentin," underglaze Coiffe mark 4, ca. 1880s, 12" h. **$1,500**

Chapter 12

Cracker Jars

Cracker jars (or biscuit jars as they are called in Europe) were produced to hold hard, cookie-like biscuits to be eaten during tea time. During the Victorian Era, when taking tea was an event, even the most utilitarian items became beautifully decorated pieces of art. Cracker jars were hand painted to match a teapot or dessert set. When it came time for a mid-morning or mid-afternoon cup of tea, out would come the tiny treasures housed in these jars.

Cracker jar, unique three handles, h.p. by unknown amateur artist, underglaze Haviland H&Co. factory mark E, 7-1/2" h............................. **$550**

Cracker jar, h.p. by unknown amateur artist using standard method of painting, underglaze T&V factory mark 7, 7-1/2" h. **$450**

Cracker jar, h.p. w/cherries, underglaze T&V factory mark 7................................ **$450**

Cracker jar, unique cov., h.p. by unknown amateur artist, underglaze T&V factory mark 8, 7-1/2" h. **$450**

Cracker jar, h.p. & signed by factory artist "Solig," underglaze Coiffe factory mark 3, overglaze Flambeau decorating mark 4, 5-1/2" h. **$550**

Cracker jar, h.p. w/roses, underglaze T&V factory mark 6. . . . . **$450**

Chapter 13

Cups and Saucers

Limoges cups and saucers were produced in the Limoges factories to be part of a dinnerware or dessert set, or part of a chocolate, tea, or coffee pot set. Many sizes from the traditional tea or coffee-cup size to a demitasse size (specifically as part of a chocolate pot set) were produced. Each cup had a matching saucer. Today, collecting a single cup and saucer has become so popular that sets are difficult to find and are priced accordingly. Punch cups were also produced and are very collectible today, and complete sets of cups and bowls are proportionately even more valuable.

Cup & saucer, h.p. by unknown amateur artist, underglaze J.P.L. factory mark 5 . . . . $50

Cup & saucer, demitasse, factory decorated, underglaze Haviland & Co. mark, overglaze Haviland France decorating mark. $50

Cup & saucer, h.p. by unknown amateur artist, underglaze Haviland factory mark 1 . . . . $80

Cup & saucer, double handled, h.p. w/burnished gold, underglaze T&V factory mark 8. . . . . $80

Cup & saucer, h.p. by unknown amateur artist, underglaze Haviland factory mark $50

Cup & saucer, h.p. by unknown amateur artist, underglaze T&V factory mark 7 . . . . $80

Cup & saucer, h.p. by unknown amateur artist, raised gold paste, underglaze Haviland factory mark
. . . . **$80**

Cup & saucer, h.p. by unknown amateur artist, raised gold paste, underglaze J.P.L. factory mark 5
. . . . **$50**

Cup & saucer, factory decorated, underglaze GDA factory mark 1, overglaze GDA decorating mark 4
. . . . **$20**

Cup & saucer, h.p. w/burnished gold, underglaze Mavaleix factory mark, overglaze marked "Healy Gold 1481" **$80**

Cup & saucer, w/dragonfly handle, underglaze Guerin factory mark 2 . . . . **$80**

Cup & saucer, w/lilacs & raised gold paste, Elite, Bawo & Dotter factory mark 11 . . . . **$80**

Cup & saucer, transfer decoration w/embellished gold, underglaze J.P.L., Pouyat factory mark 5, overglaze Pouyat decorating mark 9 . . . . **$50**

Cup & saucer, transfer decoration w/embellished gold, underglaze J.P.L., Pouyat factory mark 5 . . . . **$50**

Cup & saucer, rare overglaze Pairpoint Limoges mark **$250**

Cup & saucer, demitasse w/transfer decoration of lily of the valley & embellished gold, underglaze Limoges France factory mark 5, overglaze Bawo & Dotter decorating mark 11 . . . . **$50**

Cup & saucer, underglaze Gerard, Dufraisseix & Morel factory mark 1, overglaze Gerard, Dufraisseix & Abbot factory mark 3 . . . . **$300**

Punch cup with under plate, h.p. w/grapes & amateur artist signed "C.E. Fann," underglaze Paroutaud Freres factory mark 1 . . . . **$100**

Punch cup, h.p. w/etched burnished gold by White's Art Decorating Studio, Chicago, underglaze factory D&C mark 3, overglaze decorating mark White's Art Studio **$100**

Punch cup, h.p. w/roses & etched burnished gold, factory decorated & artist signed "B. Aubin," underglaze factory T&V mark 7, overglaze decorating mark L.R.L. mark 3 . . . .**$170**

Punch cup w/handle, h.p. w/wild roses & grapes, underglaze factory T&V mark 7 . . . . **$150**

Punch cup, h.p. w/grapes, underglaze factory T&V mark 7 . . . . **$50**

Punch cup, h.p. w/cherubs by unknown amateur artist, underglaze T&V factory mark 7 . . . . **$150**

Punch cup with underplate, w/etched burnished gold, factory decorated, underglaze & decorating Balleroy mark 1 . . . . **$200**

Chapter 14

Dessert Plates

Dessert plates, tea plates, and luncheon plates are typically from 7 to 9 inches in diameter. Smaller side plates were normally used for buns, bread, and butter. Larger plates are categorized as dinner plates. With the evolution of dining, various uses for specific sized plates followed. Many dessert plates were painted individually or as luncheon or dessert sets. Complete dessert sets are rare and include the teapot, chocolate pot, or coffee pot, and a creamer and sugar bowl. Dessert plates are very collectible and look lovely hanging on the wall individually or in a group. Beware of an Internet seller who describes a dessert plate as a charger. Chargers are 12 inches or more in diameter and were originally intended to be used on the dinner table under the service/dinner plate.

Dessert plate, 8" d., factory h.p. & artist signed "Henria," underglaze Coiffe factory mark 3, overglaze Flambeau China decorating mark 4 .... $150

Dessert plate, 8" d., factory h.p. & artist signed "Leona," underglaze J.P.L. factory mark 5, overglaze J.P.L. decorating mark 9 .... $175

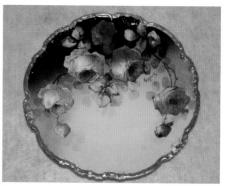

Dessert plate, 8" d., factory h.p. & artist signed "Duval," underglaze J.P.L. factory mark 5, overglaze J.P.L. decorating mark 9 .... $175

Dessert plate, 8" d., factory h.p. & artist signed "Segur," underglaze J.P.L. factory mark 5, overglaze J.P.L. decorating mark 9 .... $200

Dessert plate, 8" d., factory h.p. & artist signed "A. Bronssillon," overglaze Coronet factory mark 1 .... $250

Dessert plate, 8" d., factory decorated using mixtion technique, underglaze Mavaleix factory mark, overglaze Coronet decorating mark 1 .... $75

Dessert plate, 8" d., factory decorated using mixtion technique, underglaze T&V factory mark 7, overglaze T&V decorating mark 9
.... $75

Dessert plate, 8" d., factory h.p. & artist signed "Fiseier," underglaze J.P.L. factory mark 5, overglaze J.P.L. decorating mark 9
.... $200

Dessert plate, 9-1/2" d., factory decorated using mixtion technique, underglaze Haviland factory mark H, overglaze Haviland decorating mark in red
.... $75

Dessert plate, 8" d., factory decorated using mixtion technique, underglaze T&V factory mark 7, overglaze T&V decorating mark 9
.... $75

Dessert plate, 9" d., factory decorated using mixtion technique, underglaze T&V factory mark 7, overglaze T&V decorating mark 9
.... $75

Dessert plate, 8" d., factory decorated using mixtion technique for the roses w/heavy raised gold-paste details, underglaze Ahrenfeldt factory mark 4, overglaze Ahrenfeldt decorating mark 7
.... Set of six $1,200

Dessert plate, 9" d., h.p. in factory w/all-over roses, underglaze T&V factory mark 5a, overglaze & import mark states "Ovington Bros. France"
.... Set of six $1,300

Dessert plate, 9" d., factory h.p. & artist signed w/ illegible signature, underglaze D&C factory mark 3 .... $100

Dessert plate, 9" d., h.p. by unknown amateur artist, underglaze mark J.P.L. factory mark 5 .... $200

Dessert plate, 9" d., factory h.p. & artist signed "Patlet," underglaze Elite factory mark 5, overglaze Elite decorating mark 9 .... $225

Dessert plate, 9-1/2" d., cobalt-blue plate w/raised enamel blue & white dots w/insert of royal carriage scene, h.p. by unknown amateur artist, underglaze J.P.L. factory mark 5 .... $350

Dessert plate, 9-1/2" d., cobalt-blue plate w/raised enamel blue & white dots w/insert of lovers, horse & two dogs, h.p. by unknown amateur artist, underglaze J.P.L. factory mark 5 .... $350

Dessert plate, 8" d., h.p. & initialed "YM" by unknown amateur artist, underglaze mark J.P.L. factory mark 5 .... $100

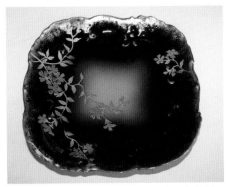

Dessert plate or ice cream bowl, 6" d., cobalt blue with raised gold gild paste, underglaze Lanternier factory mark 4, overglaze Lanternier decorating mark 6, import mark: "WL HELM & GRAFF" . . . . **Set of 12 $1,200**

Dessert plate, 8" d., impressed & overglazed Lanternier factory mark 4 . . . . **Set of eight $450**

Dessert plate, 9" d., h.p. & signed by amateur artist "M.O. MCKeown 1907," underglaze J.P.L. factory mark 5 . . . . **$100**

Dessert plate, 7" d., factory decorated, underglaze T&V factory mark 7, overglaze T&V decorating mark 9 . . . . **$75**

Dessert plate, 7-1/2" d., h.p. by unknown amateur artist, underglaze Haviland factory mark H **$50**

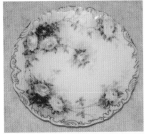

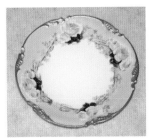

Dessert plate, 8" d., h.p. & initialed "CA" by unknown amateur artist, underglaze Klingenberg factory mark 8 . . . . **$50**

Dessert plate, 7-1/2" d., h.p. by unknown amateur artist who left initials & date "K 1896," underglaze T&V factory mark 7 . . . . **$90**

Dessert plate, 8" d., h.p. & dated "Mrs. K. Hall 1906," an unknown amateur artist, underglaze J.P.L. factory mark 5 . . . . **$75**

Dessert plate, 8" d., h.p. & signed & dated "E.E. Contwell Oct 14, 1902" an unknown amateur artist, underglaze Limoges France factory mark 2 . . . . $60

Dessert plate, 8" d., h.p. & signed "Isabel Ross," unknown amateur artist, underglaze T&V factory mark 8 . . . . $75

Dessert plate, 8-1/2" d., h.p. & signed by amateur artist "S. Morgan," underglaze J.P.L. factory mark 5 . . . . $100

Dessert plate, 8" d., h.p. w/raised enamel & gold paste, underglaze Haviland factory mark I . . . . Set of 12 $1,200

Dessert plate, 10" d., h.p. by unknown amateur artist, underglaze Haviland factory mark H . . . $200

Dessert plate, 6" d., h.p. w/ raised gold gild & enamel blue dots by unknown amateur artist, underglaze Haviland factory mark I $150

Dessert plate, 8" d., h.p. w/ raised gold gild & enamel blue dots by unknown amateur artist, underglaze Haviland factory mark I $150

Dessert plate, 8-1/2" d., h.p. & signed by amateur artist "S. Morgan," underglaze J.P.L. factory mark 5 . . . . $100

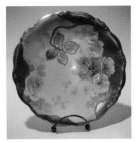

Dessert plate, 8-1/4" d., h.p., underglaze Elite, Bawo & Dotter factory mark 5, overglaze decorating mark 9 ....$200

Dessert plate, 6" h.p., underglaze Haviland factory mark I $40

Dessert plate, 8" d., h.p. w/violets, underglaze T&V factory mark 5 ....$60

Dessert plate, 10" d., h.p. by unknown amateur artist, underglaze Haviland factory mark H $200

Dessert plate, 10" d., h.p. w/etched burnished gold by White's Art Decorating Studio, Chicago, underglaze Haviland factory mark Q, overglaze decorating mark White's Art Studio........$600

Dessert plate, 8-1/2" d., h.p. & signed by amateur artist "S. Morgan," underglaze J.P.L. factory mark 5 ....$100

Dessert plate, 8-1/2" d., h.p. & signed by amateur artist "S. Morgan," underglaze J.P.L. factory mark 5 ....$100

Dessert plate, 8-1/2" d., h.p. & signed by amateur artist "S. Morgan," underglaze J.P.L. factory mark 5 ....$100

Dessert plate, 8-1/2" d., h.p. & signed by amateur artist "S. Morgan," underglaze J.P.L. factory mark 5 . . . . **$100**

Dessert plate, 6-1/2" d., h.p. w/illegible artist's initials, underglaze CFH Haviland factory mark **$90**

Dessert plate, 6-1/2" d., h.p. w/illegible artist's initials, underglaze CFH Haviland factory mark **$90**

Dessert plate, 10" d., h.p. by unknown amateur artist, J.P.L. factory mark 4 . . . . **$125**

Dessert plate, 9-1/2" d., h.p., underglaze J.P.L., Pouyat factory mark 5 . . . . **Set of four $200**

Dessert plate, 6-1/2" d., h.p. w/illegible artist's initials, underglaze CFH Haviland factory mark **$90**

Dessert plate, 6-1/2" d., h.p. w/illegible artist's initials, underglaze CFH Haviland factory mark **$90**

Dessert plate, 6-1/2" d., h.p. w/illegible artist's initials, CFH Haviland factory mark **$90**

Dessert plates, 6" d., 8" d. & matching cup & saucer, h.p. w/ raised gild & enamel blue dots by unknown amateur artist, underglaze Haviland factory mark I ....**Set $350**

Dessert plates, 6" d., 8" d. & matching cup & saucer, factory decorated w/embossed gold gild, underglaze Bernardaud factory mark 1, overglaze Bernardaud decorating mark 3 .....**Set $175**

Dessert plate, 7" d., & matching cup & saucer, h.p. & amateur artist signed & dated "J.J.Driscoll 1910," underglaze T&V factory mark 8 ....**Set $150**

Dessert plate, 9-1/2" d., h.p., underglaze J.P.L., Pouyat factory mark 5 ....**Set of six $600**

Pair of dessert plates, 7-1/2" d., h.p. & artist signed "Nyr-Felt," L. underglaze D&C factory mark 3, R. underglaze J.P.L. factory mark 5 ....**Pair $200**

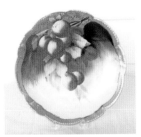

Dessert plate, 8-3/4" d., h.p. & factory artist signed "LeRoy," underglaze AK factory mark 7, overglaze Pickard decorating studio mark...........**$200**

Dessert plate, 8-1/2" d., h.p. & factory artist signed "E. Challinor," underglaze Haviland mark 12, overglaze Pickard decorating studio mark **$200**

Dessert plate, 6-1/2" d., h.p. w/ illegible artist's initials, underglaze CFH Haviland factory mark ...**$90**

Chapter 15

Dinnerware

Dinnerware is what started the massive production of Limoges porcelain in France during the 19th century. The Haviland factory is best known for its dinner and tableware in the American porcelain market, and its success between 1842 and 1855 inspired other porcelain factories in the Limoges region to export their wares. Dinnerware sets sold for $19.95 to $39.95 and included 12 dinner, dessert, salad, and bread plates, salt dishes, soup bowls, cups and saucers, bone dishes, four platters of varying sizes, two covered bowls, two uncovered vegetable bowls, soup tureen, gravy boat with under plate, and creamer and sugar. Additional pieces like the teapot, chocolate pot, or coffee pot, with matching cups and saucers, pitchers, platters, and bowls could be ordered at an additional cost.

Throughout the centuries we have seen major changes in dining habits. Today, elaborate dining and formal dinner parties are a thing of the past, and the value of antique Limoges dinnerware is at an all-time low. The dinnerware sets are functional, but they are not microwave or dishwasher safe, making the supply far exceed the demand. On the other hand, complete sets of antique dinnerware that have extensive gold, are cobalt blue or cranberry, or are hand painted and extremely decorative, are very desirable.

Dinner plate, 12" d., cobalt blue w/thick raised gold-paste accents, underglaze Ahrenfeldt factory mark 6, overglaze Ahrenfeldt decorating mark 8a . . . . Set of 12 $3,500

Salad plate, 8" d., w/thin cobalt rim, underglaze Vignaud Freres factory mark 3, Wanamaker's import mark . . . . Set of 12 $200

Dinner plate, 11" d., w/center gold medallion, underglaze Ahrenfeldt factory mark 5, overglaze Boston import mark . . . . Set of 12 $1,500

Dinner plate, 11" d., underglaze W.G.&Co., Guerin factory mark 3, overglaze Guerin decorating mark 4 . . . . Set of 12 $1,500

Dinner plate, 11" d., underglaze W.G.&Co., Guerin factory mark 3, overglaze Guerin decorating mark 4 . . . . Set of 12 $1,500

Dinner plate, 11" d., underglaze W.G.&Co., Guerin factory mark 3, overglaze Guerin decorating mark 4 . . . . Set of 12 $1,500

Platter, 9-1/2" d., 12" l., underglaze J.P.L. factory mark 5 . . $450

Dinner plate, 11" d., cobalt w/ heavy gold, underglaze W.G.&Co. factory mark 2 . . . . $200

Divided platter, 13" d., no underglaze whiteware mark, Pouyat decorating mark 3 . . . . $750

Dinner plate, 12" d., cranberry w/raised gold paste & hand painted enamel center medallion, underglaze W.G.&Co., Guerin factory mark 3, overglaze Martin's Detroit import mark . . . . . **Set of 12 $3,500**

Dinner plate, 12" d., underglaze PL, La Porcelaine Limousine factory mark 2 . . . . **Set of 12 $2,000**

Chop plate, 14" d., underglaze Limoges France factory mark 3, overglaze Blakeman & Henderson decorating mark 3 . . . . **$850**

Dinner plate, 12" d., underglaze T&V factory mark 5a, overglaze marked "Ovington Brothers" . . . . **Set of 12 $1,500**

Dinner plate, 12" d., underglaze T&V factory mark 5a. . . . . **Set of 15 $2,500**

Dinner plate, 12" d., underglaze Haviland factory mark Q . . . . **Set of 6 $300**

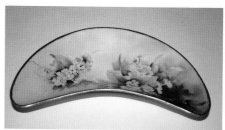

Bone dish, h.p., underglaze T&V factory mark 4a
. . . . **$80**

Bone dish, h.p., underglaze T&V factory mark 4a
. . . . **$80**

Bone dish, underglaze G.D.M. mark 2, overglaze Robert Haviland mark 3. . . . . **$25**

Bone dish, underglaze Lanternier mark 3, overglaze Lanternier decorating mark 6 . . . . **$25**

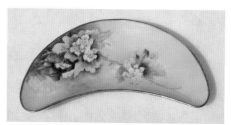

Bone dish, h.p., underglaze Guerin factory mark 3
. . . . **$100**

Bone dish, h.p., underglaze T&V factory mark 4a
. . . . **$80**

Divided serving piece, 13" d., h.p., underglaze T&V factory mark 8 . . . .**$650**

Dinner plate, 11-1/2" d., underglaze W.G.&Co. factory mark 3 . . . .**Set of eight $1,500**

Dinner plate, 11-1/2" d., underglaze W.G.&Co. factory mark 3 . . . . **Set of 10 $1,500**

Bread & butter plate, 6" d., underglaze Ahrenfeldt factory mark 6a, overglaze Ahrenfeldt 8b . . . . **Set of 12 $250**

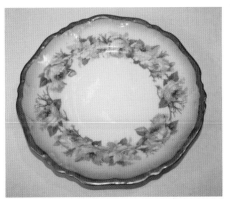

Bread & butter plate, 6" d., underglaze Laviolette factory mark 1, overglaze Klingenberg decorating mark 9. . . . . **Set of 12 $250**

Bread & butter plate, 6" d., underglaze Lanternier factory mark 4, overglaze Lanternier decorating mark 6 . . . . **Set of 12 $250**

Dessert plate, 8" d., underglaze Plainemaison factory mark 1, overglaze "Avenir" . . . . **Set of 12 $350**

Dessert or salad plate, 9-1/2", underglaze D&Co. factory mark 3, overglaze D&Co. decorating mark 5 . . . . **Set of 12 $600**

Dinnerware 93

Platter, 14" d., 20" l., h.p. w/
roses, artist signed & dated "Elva
Seyooley 1902," underglaze
Haviland factory mark H
. . . . **$1,500**

Platter, 9" d., 14" l., h.p. & artist
signed "S. Morgan," underglaze
J.P.L. factory mark 5 . . . **$1,000**

Platter, 12" d., 18" l., underglaze Haviland factory mark
F. **$900**

Platter, 14" d., 20" l., h.p. w/roses, underglaze J.P.L.
factory mark 5 . . . . **$1,200**

Covered soup tureen, 12" d., 11" h., h.p. w/roses, underglaze J.P.L. factory mark 5 . . . . **$900**

Covered soup tureen, 8" d., 9" h., h.p. w/berries & wild roses, artist signed "Andrew," underglaze Paroutaud Freres factory mark 2 . . . . **$1,500**

Covered soup tureen, 15" d., 16" h., h.p. w/courting scene, encrusted w/jewels, raised enamel & gold paste, underglaze Haviland factory mark H **$2,500**

Sauceboat w/underliner, 5" d., 6" h., underglaze Elite factory mark 5 . . . . **$250**

J.P.L. Set

Dinner service for 12: dinner plates, 11" d., salad plates, 8" d., bread & butter plates, 6" d., cups & saucers, decorated using a decal underglaze J.P.L. factory mark 5, overglaze J.P.L. decorating mark 8 . . . .**Setting for 12 $450**

Covered vegetable bowl, underglaze J.P.L. factory mark 5, overglaze J.P.L. decorating mark 8

Tiny covered tureen, underglaze J.P.L. factory mark 5, overglaze J.P.L. decorating mark 8

Three platters, underglaze J.P.L. factory mark 5, overglaze J.P.L. decorating mark 8

Dinner service for 12: dinner plate 11-1/2" d., salad plate 8-1/2" d., dessert plate 6" d., bowl 8" d., bowl 6" d., bread & butter plate 4" d., double-handled soup bowl & saucer 5-1/2" d., cup & saucer, serving pieces, etc., 1/2" gold rim, underglaze Vignaud Freres factory mark 3, overglaze Wanamaker's import mark
. . . .**Setting for 12 $1,500**

Gravy boat w/underliner, underglaze Vignaud Freres factory mark 3, overglaze Wanamaker's import mark

Covered vegetable dish, underglaze Vignaud Freres factory mark 3, overglaze Wanamaker's import mark

Double-handled soup w/saucer, underglaze Vignaud Freres factory mark 3, overglaze Wanamaker's import mark

Large soup bowl, underglaze Vignaud Freres factory mark 3, overglaze Wanamaker's import mark

Uncovered vegetable dish/bowl, underglaze Vignaud Freres factory mark 3, overglaze Wanamaker's import mark

Various platters, underglaze Vignaud Freres factory mark 3, overglaze Wanamaker's import mark

T&V/McFeely Set

Setting for 10 $3,500

Dinner plate, 10-1/2" d., h.p. & artist signed "E. Blanche McFeely," underglaze T&V Tressemann & Vogt factory mark 8

Dinner plate, 10-1/2" d., h.p. & artist signed "E. Blanche McFeely," underglaze T&V Tressemann & Vogt factory mark 8

Covered bowl, 6-1/2" d., 9" h., h.p. & artist signed "E. Blanche McFeely," underglaze T&V Tressemann & Vogt factory mark 8

Covered bowl, 7" d., 9" h., h.p. & artist signed "E. Blanche McFeely," underglaze T&V Tressemann & Vogt factory mark 8

Unique shaped bowl, 9" d., 3-1/2" h., h.p. & artist signed "E. Blanche McFeely," underglaze T&V factory mark 8

Uncovered bowl, 9" d., 5-1/2" h., h.p. & signed by amateur artist "E. Blanche McFeely," underglaze T&V factory mark 8

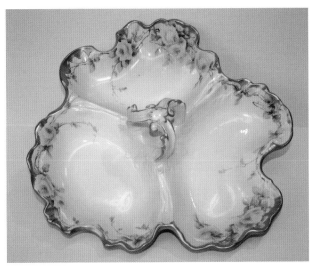

Divided serving piece, 14-1/2" d., h.p. & signed by amateur artist "E. Blanche McFeely," underglaze T&V factory mark 8

Dinnerware 99

Haviland Set

Dinner service for eight: dinner plate 11-1/2" d., salad plate 8-1/2" d., berry bowl 6" d., butter pat 1" d., cups & saucers, three serving platters, cov., soup tureen, gravy boat w/underliner, underglaze Haviland mark P, overglaze Haviland mark
. . . .**Partial set $350**

Platter, 12" l., underglaze Haviland mark P, overglaze Haviland mark

Gravy boat & underliner, underglaze Haviland mark P, overglaze Haviland mark

Tureen, underglaze Haviland mark P, overglaze Haviland mark

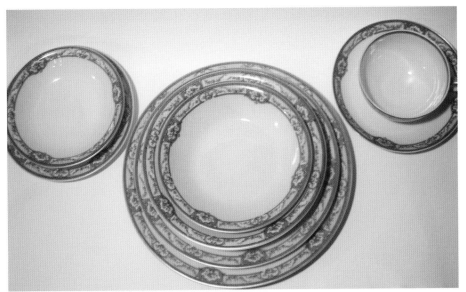

Dinner service for 12: dinner plate 11-1/2" d., salad plate 8-1/2" d., dessert plate 6" d., bowl 8" d., bowl 6" d., bread & butter plate 4" d., 5-1/2" d., cup & saucer, (not shown: three platters, three serving bowls, gravy boat, coffee & tea service, etc. over 200 pieces), Theodore Haviland factory mark P, red overglaze Haviland mark .... **Settting for 12 $800**

Dinner service for 12: dinner plates, 11" d., salad plates, 8" d., bread & butter plates, 6" d., cups & saucers, three platters, whiteware w/embossed gold 1/2" d., new old stock, underglaze Limoges France factory mark 5, not shown: vegetable bowls, tureens, etc. .... **Setting for 12 $1,500**

Haviland dinnerware set: dinner plates, 11" d., salad plates, 8" d., bread & butter plates, 6" d., marked Charles Field, Haviland, Limoges, Haviland factory mark 3 .... **Set $1,500**

Dinnerware 101

Chapter 16

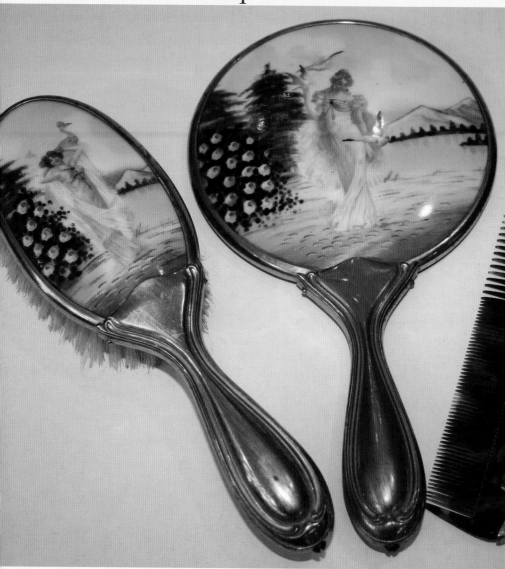

Dresser Top Accoutrements

During the Victorian Era, elegance was an integral part of the lifestyle. The Victorian woman would sit on a tufted chair or stool in front of an elegant dressing table, accompanied by a servant or a personal nursemaid, and prepare herself for the day. Beautiful hand painted trays were used to preserve the tops of furniture and could be purchased in sizes ideal for displaying a young woman's desired pieces. Complete dresser sets were typically factory decorated and included a 10- to 12-inch tray, hair receiver, powder jar, button jar, small pin tray, and sometimes a small covered box, candlesticks, and hatpin holder. Mirrors did not seem to be included in the dresser sets, but they are placed in this chapter because they are logically grouped with the other items.

Dresser set: dresser tray, powder jar & candlesticks on feet, hair receiver & pin tray, h.p. by unknown amateur artist in pastel colors & raised gold paste & enamel dots, all pieces marked underglaze PL Limoges France factory mark 1
. . . . **Set $900**

Dresser set: under tray, pin tray, cov. box, jar & jar w/feet, h.p. by unknown amateur artist who chose different blanks from different factories & h.p. as a set; pin tray underglaze T&V factory mark 7, rest of set has W.G.&Co. underglaze factory mark 2 . . . . **Set $1,200**

Dresser set: under tray, cov. box & powder jar, button jar & candlestick, h.p. by unknown amateur artist who chose different blanks from different factories & h.p. as a set; pin tray underglaze T&V factory mark 7, rest of set has W.G.&Co. underglaze factory mark 2 . . . . **Set $1,200**

Dresser set: under tray, cov. box & powder jar, hair receiver & candlesticks, h.p. by unknown amateur artist who chose blanks from the same factory, underglaze T&V factory mark 7 . . . . **Set $900**

Dresser set: under tray, cov. powder jar & hair receiver, h.p. w/violets & raised gold paste by unknown artist, underglaze J.P.L. factory mark 5 . . . . **Set $1,200**

Dresser set: under tray, cov. powder jar & hair receiver, h.p. by unknown artist, underglaze T&V factory mark 7 . . . . **Set $600**

Dresser tray w/cov. powder jar, both pieces h.p. to match, artist signed "S.C. Norrell," tray is marked w/underglaze Limoges France Plainemaison mark 1, powder jar underglaze GDA factory mark 1 . . . . **Set $450**

Dresser set: under tray, pin tray, cov. powder jar & hair receiver, h.p. by unknown artist in Pickard factory, underglaze T&V factory mark 7, overglaze Pickard mark in gold . . . . **Set $1,500**

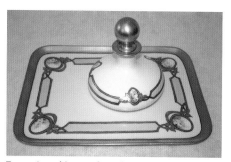

Tray w/matching perfume bottle, h.p. by unknown amateur artist, underglaze Limoges France factory mark 1. . . . . **Set $300**

Dresser tray w/hatpin holder & perfume decanter, h.p. by unknown amateur artist who picked different blanks to create a set, tray underglaze T&V factory mark 8, decanter underglaze D&C factory mark 4, hatpin holder unmarked . . . . **Set $450**

Dresser tray w/candlesticks, h.p. by unknown amateur artist, underglaze Limoges France factory mark 1
. . . . tray **$175**
. . . . candlesticks **$295**

Dresser tray, factory decorated using the mixtion technique, underglaze Coiffe factory mark 3, overglaze Flambeau decorating mark 4a, 12-1/2 x 9-1/2". . **$250**

Powder jar, h.p. w/wild roses & raised enamel, underglaze D&C factory mark 2, 6" d., 3" h. **$500**

Powder jar, h.p. w/raised enamel dots & gold scroll, underglaze Limoges France factory mark 2, 8" d., 4" h. **$500**

Powder jar, h.p. w/roses, underglaze T&V factory mark 7, 6" d., 3" h. **$300**

Powder jar, h.p. w/dark roses, underglaze Limoges France factory mark 2, 6" d., 3" h. **$300**

Powder jar, h.p. w/roses, burnished gold & raised enamel, underglaze T&V factory mark 7, 6" d., 3" h. **$500**

Powder jar, h.p. w/violets inside & out, underglaze Klingenberg factory mark 7, 8" d., 4" h. **$500**

Powder jar, transfer decoration of cherubs, no mark, 3" d., 3" h. **$250**

Powder jar, h.p. w/portrait & raised enamel, underglaze Limoges France factory mark 1, 8" d., 4" h. **$700**

Powder jar, transfer of Queen Louise w/raised enamel & blue dots, underglaze T&V factory mark 7, 8" d., 4" h.. . . . .**$200**

Dresser Top Accoutrements 107

Powder jar, h.p. w/roses, underglaze T&V factory mark 5a, 6-1/2" d., 3" h. **$300**

Hair receiver, h.p. by unknown amateur artist, underglaze W.G. France factory mark 2, 5-1/2" d., 2" h.. . . . . **$200**

Hair receiver, h.p. by unknown amateur artist w/raised enamel, underglaze W.G. France factory mark 2, 5-1/2" d., 2" h. **$250**

Two mirrors & brush, factory decorated using decal, no visible marks, ca. 1950s . . . . **Set $350**

Mirror, brush & comb set, factory h.p., gold overlay on sterling silver, no visible marks, 19th c. . . . . **Set $2,250**

Mirror, factory artist signed "Petit," original back prevents seeing manufacturing marks, 19th c., 8" l. **$700**

Mirror, factory artist signed "Murville," original back prevents seeing manufacturing marks, 19th c., 8" l.. . . . . **$700**

Mirror, factory artist signed "Petit," original back prevents seeing manufacturing marks, 19th c., 8" l. **$700**

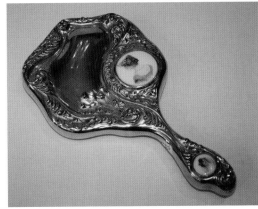

Mirror, factory artist signed "Girsard," original back prevents seeing manufacturing marks, 19th c., 8" l. **$700**

Mirror, French silver mark, w/h.p. porcelain insets of women, ca. 1910, 11" l. **$300**

Perfume or oil bottle, h.p. w/roses, underglaze UC factory mark 1, 8" h. **$120**

Mirror, comb & brush w/transfer-decorated porcelain tops, ca. 1920. . . . . **Set $200**

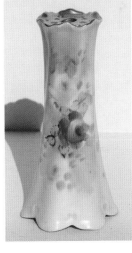

Hat pin holder, h.p. by unknown amateur artist, underglaze T&V factory mark 8, 7" h. **$250**

Perfume bottle w/o original stopper, h.p. & artist signed & dated "Jessie Davis Dec 1904," underglaze T&V factory mark 8, 6" h. **$50**

Chapter 17

Ewers

Ewers are normally 10 to 17 inches tall with an average height of 12 inches and are sometimes referred to as a pitcher. Ewers should never be compared to tankards. Ewers are decorative, curvaceous, and elaborate and are not as massive or as heavy as a tankard. In addition, ewers were never produced with matching mugs, cups, or trays, as were tankards and cider pitchers, although an amateur American artist could have decorated these items to match.

Ewer, w/four cups & tray, underglaze T&V factory mark 7, 13" h. . . . .**Set $2,000**

Ewer, rare w/h.p. reserves of figural scenes, Haviland factory artist signed & dated "A. Nice 1893" in brown, underglaze H.& C. factory mark 11 w/H.&Co. in gold script **$3,500**

Ewer, factory h.p. & artist signed "Leona," underglaze J.P.L. factory mark 5, 14-1/2" h. **$1,000**

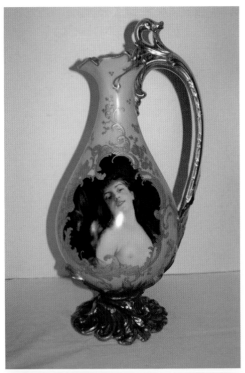

Ewer, rare w/h.p. portrait on one side, overglaze decorating Coronet factory mark 2, 15" h.. . . **$4,000**

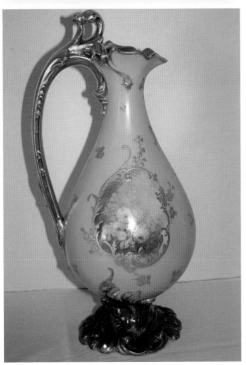

Ewer (back), w/h.p. roses, overglaze decorating Coronet factory mark 2, 15" h.

Chapter 18

Ferniers

Ferniers, also known as fern pots, are similar to jardinières and planters in function: they all hold house plants—specifically ferns—but the fernier's shape is the distinguishing feature. A fernier is oblong and stout with the average size approximately 5 inches tall by 7 to 9 inches in diameter. Ferniers originally had an insert with holes. The insert acted as a liner for the pot and a drain for the plant. The plant would be placed directly on top of the liner so it never sat in the accumulated water. Over the years, these liners have frequently been broken or misplaced, so any type of planter with its original liner is very rare and desirable.

Fernier, 10" d., 8" h., h.p. w/scene on both sides, underglaze d'Albis & Romanet factory mark 1, overglaze decorating studio Bawo & Dotter factory mark 9a. **$1,500**

Fernier, 8" d., 5" h., h.p. by unknown amateur artist, underglaze Limoges France. **$500**

Fernier, 10" d., 8" h., h.p. w/roses, underglaze d'Albis & Romanet factory mark 1, overglaze decorating studio Bawo & Dotter mark 9a **$1,500**

Fernier, 9" d., 5-1/2" h., h.p. w/roses & raised gold, underglaze D&C factory mark 3 . . . . **$1,200**

Fernier, 8" d., 5" h., factory decorated using mixtion, underglaze AK factory mark 8, overglaze decorating studio mark 9 . . . . **$300**

Fernier, 9" d., 5-1/2" h., h.p. w/roses, underglaze D&C factory mark 3 . . . . **$900**

Fernier, 9" d., 5-1/2" h., h.p. w/violets & burnished gold feet, underglaze D&C factory mark 3 . . . . **$800**

Fernier, 8" d., 5" h., h.p. w/cameo of roses, outlined in black w/black feet, underglaze Limoges France factory mark 6 . . . . **$700**

Fernier, 9"d., 4-1/2" h. factory decorated, underglaze T&V factory mark 7, overglaze T&V decorating studio mark 16 . . . . **$700**

Fernier w/original frog insert, 10" d., 5-1/2" h., h.p. by unknown artist, underglaze T&V factory mark 7 . . . . **$1,200**

Fernier w/blown out blank detail on edge, h.p. & outlined in black, illegible signature & dated "1907," underglaze T&V factory mark 5 . . . . **$650**

Footed fernier w/original liner, 10" d., 5-1/2" h., underglaze Limoges France factory mark 6 . . . . **$1,500**

Ferniers 117

Chapter 19

Fish Sets and Oyster Plates

Eating during the Victorian Era was an elaborate event. Courses were served one after another on plates specifically designed for the type of food being served. Fish platters were over 22 inches long to allow for all types of fish from cod to salmon to be elegantly served. Complete fish sets would include the platter, plates, and sauceboat. Other individual pieces such as oyster plates, dishes, sardine boxes, etc. were hand painted or decorated with a seafood motif.

Fish set: platter 10" d., 19" l., w/12 matching plates, 10" d., h.p. & artist signed "Duval," underglaze J.P.L. factory mark 5 . . . . **Set $3,500**

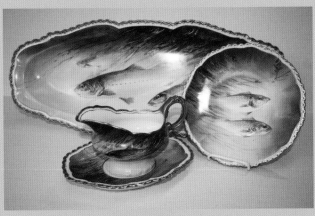

Fish set: platter 10" d., 19" l., sauceboat w/ underliner, 10 plates 10" d., h.p. & artist signed "Engreval," underglaze J.P.L. factory mark 5 . . . . **Set $3,500**

Fish platter, 10-1/2" d., 20" l., factory h.p., embossed w/T&H mark M in whiteware, overglaze decorating Theodore Haviland mark q **$2,000**

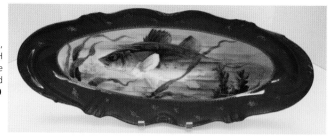

Fish platter, 10" d., 24" l., h.p. & signed by factory artist "DeLarfeuil," underglaze Limoges France Plainemaison factory mark 1, Lewis Straus & Sons overglaze decorating studio mark 1 . . . . **$1,200**

Oyster plate, underglaze Gerard, Dufraisseix & Morel factory mark 2, overglaze Gerard, Dufraisseix & Abbot decorating mark 3 . . . .**Set of six $495**

Oyster plate, 10" d., underglaze Bawo & Dotter factory mark 2 . . . .**$250**

Oyster plate, 11" d., underglaze Limoges France factory mark 7 .... **$600**

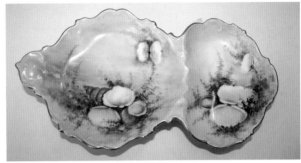

Sardine tray, 6" d., 10" l., h.p. & artist signed by amateur artist "H.D.A. Hearn," underglaze T&V factory mark 8 .... **$450**

Sardine tray w/matching box, tray 6" d., 10-1/2" l., box 3" d., 6" l., both h.p. by unknown artist, underglaze T&V factory mark 7 .... **Set $950**

Fish tray, 8" d., 12" l., h.p. by unknown amateur artist, underglaze Haviland France factory mark **$350**

Fish plaque, 12" d., hand painted in factory & artist signed "Dubois," underglaze Flambeau factory mark 1, overglaze Flambeau decorating mark 3 .... **$650**

Chapter 20

Game Sets

The game course consisted of wild game such as pheasant, quail, deer, or boar and was served on a platter with matching plates at the appropriate time of the meal. This platter is oval and not as long as a fish platter, making it conducive to serving a red meat. Ten to 12 matching plates of approximately 9 to 10 inches in diameter and a sauceboat would be included in a complete game set.

Game platter, 16" d., 20" l., h.p. center, desired cobalt-blue rim w/burnished gold embellishments, J.P.L. Pouyat factory mark 5 . . . . **$3,500**

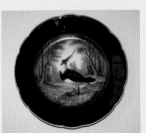  

Game plate, cobalt blue, 8" d., h.p. in factory, underglaze CFH, GDM factory mark 1, overglaze script R. B. in red. **$250**

Game plate, cobalt blue, 8" d., h.p. in factory, underglaze CFH, GDM factory mark 1, overglaze script R. B. in red. **$250**

Game plate, cobalt blue, 8" d., h.p. in factory, underglaze CFH, GDM factory mark 1, overglaze script R. B. in red **$250**

Game plate, cobalt blue, 8" d., h.p. in factory, underglaze CFH, GDM factory mark 1, overglaze script R. B. in red. **$250**

Game plate, cobalt blue, 8" d., h.p. in factory, underglaze CFH, GDM factory mark 1, overglaze script R. B. in red. **$250**

Game platter, 16" d., 20" l., h.p. in factory & artist signed "Duval," underglaze Klingenberg factory mark 7, overglaze Klingenberg decorating mark 9 (Part of a set that includes eight plates, six of which are shown in following photos) . . . . **Set $4,500**

Game plate (part of the set that includes platter & eight plates), 9" d., h.p. in factory & artist signed "Duval," underglaze Klingenberg factory mark 7, overglaze Klingenberg decorating mark 9 . . . .**Set $4,500**

Game plate (part of the set that includes platter & eight plates), 9" d., h.p. in factory & artist signed "Duval," underglaze Klingenberg factory mark 7, overglaze Klingenberg decorating mark 9 . . . .**Set $4,500**

Game plate (part of the set that includes platter & eight plates), 9" d., h.p. in factory & artist signed "Duval," underglaze Klingenberg factory mark 7, overglaze Klingenberg decorating mark 9. . . . .**Set $4,500**

Game plate (part of the set that includes platter & eight plates), 9" d., h.p. in factory & artist signed "Duval," underglaze Klingenberg factory mark 7, overglaze Klingenberg decorating mark 9. . . . .**Set $4,500**

Game plate (part of the set that includes platter & eight plates), 9" d., h.p. in factory & artist signed "Duval," underglaze Klingenberg factory mark 7, overglaze Klingenberg decorating mark 9. . . . .**Set $4,500**

Game plate (part of the set that includes platter & eight plates), 9" d., h.p. in factory & artist signed "Duval," underglaze Klingenberg factory mark 7, overglaze Klingenberg decorating mark 9. . . . .**Set $4,500**

Game platter, 14" d., 20" l., h.p. by unknown amateur artist, underglaze T&V factory mark 4 . . . . **$1,500**

Game platter, 13" d., 19" l., h.p. & factory artist signed "E. Goumondie," burnished gold, underglaze W.G.&Co. factory mark 2, overglaze Wm. Guerin & Co. decorating mark 4 ...... **$3,000**

Game platter, 15" d., 18" l., h.p. & factory artist signed "Dubois," raised gold paste, underglaze Coiffe factory mark 2 .... **$3,000**

Game platter, 12" d., 19" l., h.p. with duck & burnished gold, underglaze Haviland factory mark F................... **$2,000**

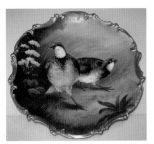

Game plaque, 10" d., h.p. & factory artist signed "Bronsillion," burnished gold rim, underglaze Coronet, Borgfeldt factory mark 1 & black label "Mellon & Hewes Co., Hartford, CT."..........**$1,000**

Game plaque, 18" d., h.p. & factory artist signed "Bronsillion," burnished gold rim, underglaze W.G.&Co., factory mark 3, overglaze Guerin decorating mark 4 ....**$3,000**

Game plaque, 10" d., h.p. & factory artist signed "DeNerval," burnished gold rim, overglaze Lazeyras, Rosenfeld & Lehman factory mark 3 ....**$1,500**

Game plaque, 14" d., h.p. & factory artist signed "Dubois," burnished gold rim, underglaze W.G.&Co., factory mark 3, overglaze Guerin decorating mark 4 ......**$2,500**

Game plaque, 13" d., h.p. & factory artist signed "Dubois," burnished gold rim, Lewis Straus & Sons factory mark 1 & "LAPWING" in gold.....**$2,500**

Game plaque, 10" d., h.p. by factory artist, underglaze LRL factory mark 1 ....**$1,000**

Game charger, 11-1/2" d., h.p. & signed by factory artist "Bronsillon," underglaze C. et J. factory mark 1 ....**$450**

Game Sets 127

Chapter 21

Inkwells and Deskware

During the Victorian Era, a lady's writing desk was where a lady would spend most of the day. Some of the duties of the lady of the house included writing assignments, practicing penmanship, corresponding to friends and family, and handwriting invitations. Penmanship was an art form, and we see elaborate and sometimes unreadable cursive writing. It is no wonder that we see a combination of their passion for china painting and passion for writing evolve into elaborate and beautiful hand painted inkwells and desk sets.

Inkwell with bronze, marked "France," ca. 1900, 6" d., 5" h.............................. **$1,200**

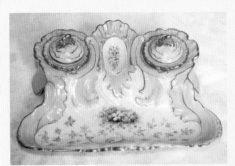

Inkwell, h.p. by amateur artist signed & dated "S.M.P. 1902," underglaze T&V factory mark 5a, 8" d., 7" h.
.... **$450**

Inkwell, h.p. by unknown artist, underglaze Limoges France factory mark 1, 8" d., 7" h. **$450**

Inkwell, h.p. by unknown artist w/raised gold paste, underglaze Limoges France factory mark 1, 8" d., 7" h.
.... **$450**

Inkwell, h.p. by unknown artist w/raised gold paste, underglaze Limoges France factory mark 1, 8" d., 7" h.
.... **$450**

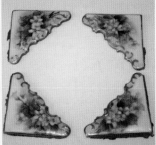

Desk set: desk corners, pen holder, ink well w/cov., h.p. w/violets, underglaze T&V factory mark 7, 19th c.
.... **Set $900**

Desk set/corners, h.p. by unknown artist, underglaze T&V factory mark 7 ... **Set $350**

Letter holder, h.p. w/roses & raised gold paste by unknown artist, underglaze Limoges France factory mark 1, 2" d., 7" h.. .... **$650**

Chapter 22

Jardinières

Originally the Limoges jardinière was intended to hold ferns and plants. Bulbous in shape, jardinières run from a diminutive 4 inches to a mammoth 18 to 20 inches across. Some of the blanks had feet and ornate handles, some had lion or elephant handles, and some came with a separate base. Most were imported as a blank and hand painted by the amateur American artist. Today, these large and beautiful pieces make breathtaking decorative statements in any home.

Jardinière, h.p. w/gold handles & feet, underglaze D&C factory mark 3, 16" d., 11" h. **$4,000**

Jardinière, h.p. w/gold handles & feet, underglaze D&C factory mark 3, 16" d., 11" h. **$4,000**

Jardinière (front, left; back, right) w/handles & feet, h.p. w/large roses, underglaze D&C factory mark 3, 16" d., 11" h.
. . . .**$3,500**

Jardinière (front, left; back, right) w/handles & feet, h.p. w/roses & gold, black outline, underglaze D&C factory mark 3, 16" d., 11" h. **$4,000**

Jardinière w/lion-head handles on separate base, h.p. w/dark roses & gold rim, handles & base, underglaze D&C factory mark 1, 14" d., 12" h.
. . . .**$4,000**

Jardinière w/lion-head handles on separate base, h.p. w/roses & gold rim, handles & base, underglaze D&C factory mark 1, 10" d., 8" h. **$3,000**

Jardinière w/lion-head handles on separate base, h.p. w/roses & burnished gold rim, handles & feet, underglaze D&C factory mark 1, 10" d., 8" h. **$2,500**

Jardinière w/lion-head handles on separate base, h.p. w/roses & raised gold-paste scrollwork, gold rim, handles & base, underglaze D&C factory mark 1, 14" d., 12" h.
. . . .**$3,000**

Jardinière w/lion-head handles on separate base, h.p. w/roses & raised gold-paste scrollwork, gold rim, handles & feet, underglaze D&C factory mark 1, 15" d., 12" h.
. . . .**$4,500**

Jardinière w/lion-head handles on separate base, h.p. w/roses & gold rim, handles & feet, raised gold paste, underglaze D&C factory mark 3, 14" d., 12" h.
. . . .**$4,000**

Jardinière w/lion-head handles on separate base, h.p. w/roses & gold rim & handles, underglaze D&C factory mark 1, 14" d., 12" h. $4,000

Jardinière w/lion-head handles on separate base, h.p. w/roses & gold handles & feet, underglaze D&C factory mark 1, 14" d., 12" h. $4,000

Jardinière w/elephant-head handles on separate base, h.p. w/pink roses & gold rim, handles & feet of base raised gold paste, underglaze D&C factory mark 3, 12" d., 11" h. $3,500

Jardinière w/elephant-head handles on separate base, h.p. w/pink roses & gold rim, handles & feet of base, raised gold paste, underglaze D&C factory mark 1, 14" d., 15" h. $4,500

Jardinière w/elephant-head handles on separate base, h.p. w/pink roses & gold rim, handles & feet of base, underglaze D&C factory mark 1, 12" d., 11" h. $2,500

Jardinière w/elephant-head handles on separate base, h.p. w/burnished gold & gold rim, handles & feet of base, outlined in black, underglaze D&C factory mark 1, 14" d., 15" h. $4,500

Jardinière on separate base, h.p. & artist signed by "Dunn," w/burnished gold rim & base, underglaze T&V factory mark 7, 9" d., 11-1/2" h. **$3,500**

Jardinière on separate base, h.p. w/burnished gold rim & base, underglaze J.P.L. factory mark 5, 41-1/2" circumference, 11" d., 13" h. **$3,500**

Jardinière (front, left; back, right) on separate base, h.p. w/cherubs, burnished gold rim & base, underglaze J.P.L. factory mark 5, 41-1/2" circumference, 11" d., 13" h. **$3,500**

Jardinière on separate base, h.p. w/dark roses, burnished gold rim & base, underglaze J.P.L. factory mark 5, 41-1/2" circumference, 11" d., 13" h. **$3,500**

Jardinière on separate base, h.p. w/burnished gold rim & base, gold enameled scroll, underglaze T&V factory mark 7, 9" d., 11-1/2" h. **$2,500**

Jardinière on unique base, h.p. w/clematis, burnished gold rim & base trim, gold enameled scroll, underglaze T&V factory mark 7, 11-1/2" d., 11" h........ **$2,500**

Jardinière on unique base, h.p. w/burnished gold scroll on rim & gold base trim, underglaze D&C factory mark 1, 11" d., 12" h........................ **$3,000**

Jardinière, h.p. underglaze T&V factory mark 7, 9" d., 9" h................................. **$1,000**

Jardinière w/elephant handles & under liner, underglaze J.P.L. Pouyat factory mark 5, 9" d., 8" h....... **$1,200**

Jardinière on unique base, h.p. w/minimum gold, underglaze D&C factory mark 1, 11" d., 12" h. **$3,000**

Jardinière on separate base, h.p. w/burnished gold base, underglaze T&V factory mark 7, 9" d., 11-1/2" h. **$2,500**

Jardinière on unique base, h.p., no gold, underglaze D&C factory mark 1, 11" d., 12" h. **$3,000**

Jardinière on separate base, h.p., raised scrolled gold & gold feet, underglaze D&C factory mark 1, 9" d., 11" h. **$3,000**

Jardinière on separate base, h.p., burnished gold scroll & gold feet, underglaze D&C factory mark 1, 11" d., 12" h. **$2,000**

Jardinière on separate base, h.p., burnished gold scroll & gold feet, underglaze D&C factory mark 1, 11" d., 12" h. **$3,000**

Jardinière on separate base, h.p. w/pastel roses, raised enamel scrolled gold & gold feet, underglaze D&C factory mark 1, 11" d., 12" h. **$3,500**

Jardinière on separate base, h.p. w/pastel roses, raised enamel scrolled gold & gold feet, underglaze D&C factory mark 1, 11" d., 12" h. **$3,500**

Jardinière, h.p. & Pickard artist signed "Osborne" poppies, underglaze T&V factory mark 7, 11" d., 12" h.
.... **$4,500**

Jardinière on separate base, h.p. w/detail, burnished gold scroll on rim w/black lines & gold feet, underglaze D&C factory mark 3, 11" d., 12" h. **$3,500**

Jardinière on separate base, h.p. w/burnished gold & black lining, underglaze D&C factory mark 1, 9" d., 11" h. **$2,000**

Jardinière on unique base, h.p. w/burnished gold scroll base, underglaze D&C factory mark 1, 11" d., 12" h. **$4,000**

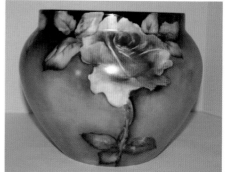

Jardinière on separate base, h.p. w/pastel roses, raised enamel blue & white dots & burnished gold, underglaze D&C factory mark 1, 6" d., 7" h. **$3,500**

Jardinière, h.p. w/roses, underglaze T&V factory mark 7, 9" d., 9-1/2" h. **$2,500**

Jardinière, h.p. w/roses, burnished gold rim, underglaze W.G.&Co., factory mark 3, 8" d., 5-1/2" h. . . . **$1,500**

Jardinière, h.p. in pastels, underglaze D&C factory mark 1, 11" d., 12" h.. . . . . **$1,000**

Jardinière, h.p. w/pastel mums & ocean scene w/ boat, underglaze D&C factory mark 1, 11" d., 12" h. **$1,000**

Jardinière, h.p. w/pastel roses & raised gold-paste scroll, underglaze D&C factory mark 1, 11" d., 12" h. **$1,000**

Jardinière, h.p. w/roses, underglaze D&C factory mark 1, 11" d., 12" h.. . . . . **$900**

Jardinière, h.p. w/cherubs & burnished gold rim, underglaze D&C factory mark 1, 11" d., 12" h. **$1,000**

Jardinière, h.p. w/dark roses, underglaze D&C factory mark 1, 6" d., 5-1/2" h. **$800**

Jardinière, h.p. w/yellow roses, underglaze W.G.&Co mark 3, 3-1/2" d., 4" h. **$450**

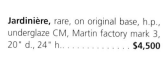

Jardinière, rare, on original base, h.p., underglaze CM, Martin factory mark 3, 20" d., 24" h. **$4,500**

Jardinière, (front, left; back, right), h.p. in factory w/courting scene, underglaze T&V factory mark 5a, overglaze T&V decorating mark 11, 7" d., 8" h. **$2,000**

Jardinière, unique blank, h.p. w/twisted handles, on attached fluted pedestal base, J.P.L. Pouyat factory mark 5, 12" d., 14" h.
. . . . **$2,500**

Jardinière, rare, w/o original base, no marks, 20" d., 19" h.. . . . . **$2,000**

Jardinière footed w/handles, h.p. w/courting couple, embellished w/burnished gold underglaze T&V mark 5a, 11" d., 12" h.. . . . . **$3,000**

Jardinière (front, left; back, right) footed w/handles, h.p. w pastel roses inside a reserve, underglaze T&V mark 5a, 11" d., 12" h.. . . . .**$3,000**

Chapter 23

Lamps

In the 19th century, Limoges factories produced oil-burning types of porcelain lamps. By 1910 and pre-World War I, most homes had electricity and began using the type of lamp with which we all are familiar. While there are many examples of Limoges lamps, in the 1920s it was popular to make a lamp out of a vase blank by having it professionally wired and placed on a base. Converted vases made into lamps are very desirable, but factory-produced Limoges oil lamps in original condition are desired by porcelain and lamp collectors alike.

Lamp, converted from vase, h.p., underglaze W.G.&Co., factory mark 2, 22" h. **$3,000**

Lamp, h.p., artist signed "Rene," underglaze W.G.&Co., factory mark 3, 24" h. **$1,000**

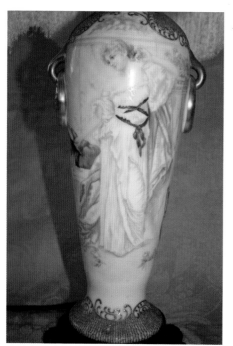

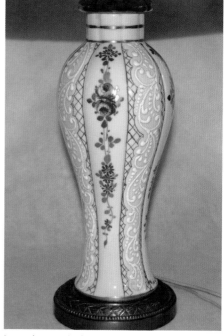

Lamp, converted from vase, h.p., underglaze W.G.&Co., factory mark 3, 14" h. **$1,000**

Lamp, h.p. w/raised enamel & tiny flowers, underglaze "France" factory mark, 12" h. **$900**

Lamp, converted from vase, h.p., underglaze T&V factory mark 8, 16" h. **$1,000**

Lamp, converted from vase, h.p., underglaze W.G.&Co., factory mark 3, 28" h. **$1,000**

Lamp, converted from vase, h.p., underglaze W.G.&Co., factory mark 2, 22" h. **$3,000**

Lamp, converted from vase, no discernible mark, 14" h. **$1,000**

Chapter 24

Miniatures

Although Limoges miniatures are not considered antique, they are popular. Some authors categorize new Limoges boxes as "miniatures" because they became popular around the mid-1980s. Most miniatures, other than the boxes, were produced from the 1950s and later. Polychrome (multiple color) pieces were produced after World War II, circa 1950s to 1980s, specifically for the American market and tourists. Cobalt blue miniatures began to flood the market in the 1980s and 1990s. Miniatures do not have a Limoges factory mark but may have the words "Limoges France" or the "Castel France" mark. The boxes may also be marked "peint a main" (hand painted) or "rehausse" (embellished by hand). The decoration on the cobalt and polychrome miniatures are created by a decal or transfer. Polychrome pieces display copies of an original painting by a famous artist. That artist's signature may be on the piece, but it is incorrect to assume it is an original.

Miniature cobalt-blue plate, 3-1/2" d., "The Progress of Love" scene, transferware decoration, marked "Limoges Castel France," ca. 1980s & after **$20**
Miniature cobalt-blue pitcher, 2" h. **& vase**, 1-5/8" h., ca. 1990s . . . . **Pair $20**

Miniature polychrome egg, marked "Limoges France" in green, ca. 1970s, 1" d., 1/2" h. **$20**

Miniature polychrome piano, marked "Limoges France peint a main," ca. 1980s, 3-1/2" l., 3" h. **$30**

Miniature perfume bottle, bottle glass w/polychrome porcelain inset marked "Limoges France," ca. 1980s, 2-1/2" h., 1" d. **$50**

Chapter 25

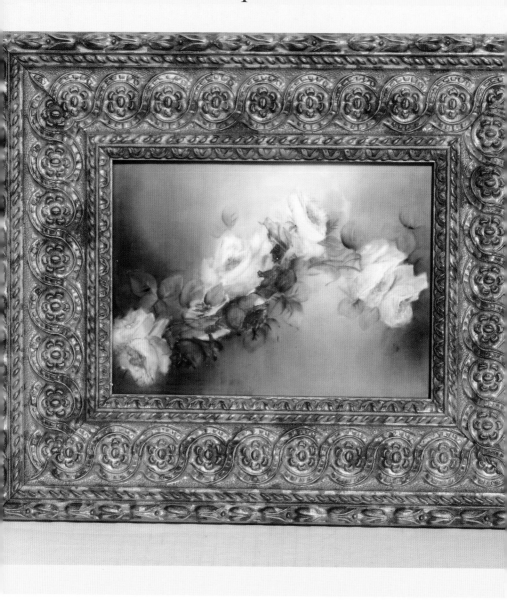

Painting on Porcelain

The King's Porcelain Manufacturing Company (KPM) in Germany produced the majority of true paintings on porcelain. Beautiful ceramic tiles were produced in England, Germany, and America that were used as fireplace surrounds or framed and sold as pieces of art. The Limoges factories produced flat pieces of porcelain from 3-by-5-inches to larger pieces of almost 30 inches to be used like a canvas by the studio and amateur artist. Most of these pieces of porcelain were produced in the Tressemann & Vogt factory and have the mark "T&V Limoges" on the back. Thousands of flat blank pieces of porcelain were exported to America and hand painted by amateur artists. A few were hand painted in the factories and are very desirable to collectors. Today, Limoges paintings on porcelain are considered pieces of art and have become excellent investments. NOTE: The dimensions annotated in the following photographs are for the porcelain only and do not include the dimension of the frame.

Painting on porcelain, h.p. by amateur artist, underglaze T&V factory mark 5a, 12" w., 9" h.
. . . . **$2,000**

Painting on porcelain, h.p. by amateur artist, underglaze T&V factory mark 5a, 5" w., 3" h.
. . . . **$900**

Painting on porcelain, h.p. by amateur artist, underglaze T&V factory mark 5a, 5" w., 7" h.
. . . . . **$1,500**

Painting on porcelain, h.p. by amateur artist, underglaze J.P.L. factory mark 5, 12" w., 9" h.
. . . . **$1,500**

Painting on porcelain, h.p. by amateur artist, underglaze D&Co. factory mark 3, 4-1/2" w., 6" h.
. . . . **$900**

Painting on porcelain, h.p. by amateur artist, underglaze T&V factory mark 5a, 5" w., 5" h. . . **$800**

Painting on porcelain, h.p. by amateur artist, underglaze J.P.L. factory mark 5, 7-1/2" d. **$1,500**

Painting on porcelain, h.p. amateur artist, in original round ornate frame, underglaze J.P.L. factory mark 1, 9" d. **$1,500**

Painting on porcelain, h.p. amateur artist, underglaze T&V factory mark 5a, 7" w., 5" h. **$1,000**

Painting on porcelain, h.p. amateur artist, underglaze T&V factory mark 5a, 5" w., 5" h. **$800**

Painting on porcelain, h.p. amateur artist, underglaze T&V factory mark 5, 4-1/2" w., 6" h. **$900**

Painting on porcelain, h.p. by amateur artist, underglaze T&V factory mark 5a, 5" w., 7" h. . . **$1,000**

Painting on porcelain, exquisite detail, h.p. & signed by factory artist "Baumy," underglaze T&V factory mark 5a, 24" d.. **$6,500**

Painting on porcelain, h.p. by amateur artist w/initials "E.L.C.," underglaze T&V factory mark 5a, 18" d. **$3,500**

Painting on porcelain, exquisite detail & enameling h.p. w/artist initials "AL" on top of "Rembrandt," overglaze Haviland decorating mark p, 18" d. **$6,500**

Painting on porcelain, h.p. & signed by American studio artist "Van," underglaze T&V factory mark 5a, overglaze "Van's China Studio 6143 S. Halsted St., Chicago, Ill.," 20" d.. . . . . **$3,500**

Painting on porcelain, enamel h.p. in factory, signed "R-BLANCER-LIMOGES," original frame & back untouched, did not remove to authenticate marks, 9" w., 8" h. **$4,000**

Painting on porcelain, in brass frame, h.p. by amateur artist, underglaze T&V factory mark 5, 5" w., 7" h. **$1,500**

Painting on porcelain, h.p. by amateur artist, underglaze T&V factory mark 5, 10" w., 12" h. **$1,500**

Painting on porcelain, h.p. in Art Nouveau style by amateur artist, underglaze T&V factory mark 7, 6" w., 14" h. **$1,500**

Painting on porcelain, h.p. in Art Nouveau style (note the addition of burnished gold) by amateur artist, underglaze T&V factory mark 7, 6" w., 14" h. **$1,600**

Painting on porcelain, h.p. by amateur artist, underglaze T&V factory mark 5, 5" w., 7" h. . . **$1,500**

Painting on porcelain, h.p. by amateur artist, underglaze T&V factory mark 7, 8" w., 12" h. . . . **$2,000**

Painting on porcelain, h.p. by amateur artist, underglaze T&V factory mark 7, 8" w., 12" h. . . **$2,000**

Painting on porcelain, "Four Seasons," four individual paintings on porcelain (Winter, Spring, Summer, Fall), 5" d., 6" h., each has artist's initials "HFM," underglaze W.G.&Co. factory mark 3, 12-1/2" w., 16" h.. . **$4,000**

Painting on porcelain, in original wood frame, underglaze Haviland factory mark E, 16" d. **$650**

Painting on porcelain, in original wood frame, underglaze Haviland factory mark E, 16" d. **$650**

Painting on porcelain, h.p. by amateur artist, underglaze T&V factory mark 7, 8" w., 12" h. **$2,000**

Painting on porcelain, h.p. & signed by factory artist "A. Nice," underglaze T&V factory mark 7, 10" w., 14" h. **$4,000**

Painting on porcelain, "Le Premier Pas," artist signed "T. Fromentin," underglaze B&Cie, mark 1, 12" w., 14" h. **$3,000**

Painting on porcelain, h.p. by amateur artist, underglaze T&V factory mark 7, 7" w., 9" h. . . **$2,500**

Painting on porcelain, original frame, decorated in factory by unknown artist, underglaze T&V factory mark 7, 14" d. **$7,500**

Painting on porcelain, h.p. by amateur artist, underglaze T&V factory mark 7, 7" w., 9" h. . **$2,500**

Painting on porcelain, h.p. amateur artist, underglaze T&V factory mark 7, 7" w., 9" h. **$800**

Painting on porcelain w/ five individual paintings, 4" d., 10" h., original frame, signed "H. Pendelton," underglaze T&V factory mark 7, 14" w., 13" h. **$6,500**

Painting on porcelain, h.p., underglaze T&V factory mark 5a, 10" w., 14" h. **$2,500**

Painting on porcelain, h.p. by amateur artist, underglaze T&V factory mark 5, 5" w., 7" h. . . **$1,500**

Painting on porcelain, h.p. w/cherubs, artist signed "A. Jolin Perreault," underglaze T&V factory mark 5, 12" w., 10" h. **$3,500**

Painting on porcelain, h.p. by amateur artist, underglaze T&V factory mark 5, 5" w., 7" h. **$1,500**

Painting on porcelain, curved, enamel, h.p. in factory, signed, original frame & back untouched, did not remove to authenticate marks, 24" w., 32" h. **$7,000**

Painting on porcelain, original frame, h.p. & signed by factory artist "a'Paroy," underglaze T&V factory mark 4b, 17" w., 18" h. . . .**$4,500**

Painting on porcelain, original frame, illegible French artist's signature, underglaze T&V factory mark 4b, 12-1/2" w., 17" h. . . . **$3,000**

Painting on porcelain, original frame, illegible French artist's signature, dated "1889," underglaze T&V factory mark 4b, 12-1/2" w., 17" h. **$3,000**

Painting on porcelain, h.p. tropical orchids attributed to Martin Johnson Heade, underglaze T&V factory mark 7, 17" w., 14" h. . . . . **$10,000+**

Painting on porcelain, artist signed & dated "Ann 1898," underglaze T&V factory mark 7, 14" w., 17" h.
. . . . **$3,000**

Painting on porcelain, h.p. w/artist's initials & dated "N.N. 1915," underglaze T&V factory mark 7, 14" w., 6" h.. . . . . **$1,500**

Painting on porcelain, underglaze T&V factory mark 7, 14" w., 11" h.. . . . . **$3,000**

Painting on porcelain, underglaze T&V factory mark 7, 15" d.. . . . . **$900**

Painting on porcelain, underglaze T&V factory mark 7, 18" d.. . . . . **$1,000**

Painting on porcelain, underglaze T&V factory mark 5b, 14" d.. . . . . **$1,500**

Painting on porcelain, underglaze T&V factory mark 5b, 14" d. **$1,500**

Painting on porcelain, underglaze T&V factory mark 5b, 14" d. **$1,500**

Painting on porcelain, h.p. mums, underglaze T&V factory mark 5b, 16" d. **$1,500**

Painting on porcelain, h.p. grapes, underglaze T&V factory mark 5b, 12" d. **$500**

Painting on porcelain, original frame, underglaze T&V factory mark 4b, 24" d. **$3,500**

Painting on porcelain, original frame, underglaze T&V factory mark 4b, 24" d. **$4,500**

Painting on porcelain, original frame, unmarked, 5" w., 3" h. **$3,500**

Painting on porcelain, underglaze W.G.&Co., factory mark 3, 18" w., 10" h. **$5,000**

Painting on porcelain, underglaze T&V factory mark 4b, 12" w., 12" h. **$500**

Painting on porcelain, underglaze T&V factory mark 4b, 12" w., 12" h. **$500**

Painting on porcelain, h.p. by amateur artist, underglaze T&V factory mark 5a, 7" w., 9-1/2" h. . . . **$2,000**

Painting on porcelain, h.p. by amateur artist, underglaze T&V factory mark 4b, 11" w., 8-1/2" h., ... **$1,500**

Chapter 26

Personal Items

Limoges was produced during the Victorian Era when it was the norm to decorate with opulence and to give in to indulgence. Useful and personal items such as wash bowls, spittoons, humidors, picture frames, and smoking items were produced in the French porcelain factories and sold to the wealthy. During this time, painting on porcelain had become a huge cottage industry. Some practical items were imported to the United States as blanks and hand painted by an amateur artist to satisfy "her" particular taste. It was the artist's objective to make an everyday item a piece of art. These amateur artists are the reason for the many variations in paint color and styles. Each piece is as unique as the artist who painted it.

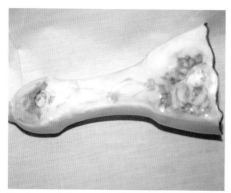

Tussie mussie, h.p., underglaze AK Klingenberg factory mark 7 . . . . **$600**

Tea caddy, h.p. w/gold gilt reserve & Victorian woman, bottom states "November 16, 1898, M.R.W. to H.B.G.," underglaze Ahrenfeldt factory mark 6 . . . . **$900**

Thermometer holder, used as frame, h.p., underglaze J.P.L. factory mark 3 . . . . **$600**

Picture frame (matches thermometer holder), h.p., underglaze J.P.L. factory mark 3 . . . . **$800**

Ladies spittoon or cuspidor, h.p. w/roses, underglaze Haviland factory mark D **$900**

Match holder, striker on bottom, artist signed & dated "M.E.B. Hutchins 1907," underglaze D&Co. factory mark 3 . . . .**$650**

Picture frame, h.p. w/forget-me-nots, underglaze J.P.L. factory mark 3 . . . .**$375**

Match box & cigarette holder, h.p., underglaze AK Klingenberg factory mark 7 . . . . **$800**

Wash pitcher w/basin, factory decorated w/burnished gold & raised enamel blue dots, underglaze Haviland factory mark I, overglaze Frank Haviland decorating mark **$4,500**

Chapter 27

Planters

A planter is another name used for a pot made specifically to house a plant. A true planter is less ostentatious, and although it may have handles, they are very small, unlike the large ornate handles of a jardinière. A planter, like a jardinière, may sit on a base, but a planter never had a liner like a fernier and was usually much larger.

Planter on base, h.p. w/roses, underglaze D&Co. factory mark 3, 16" h. **$2,000**

Planter, h.p. w/roses, underglaze D&Co. factory mark 3, 7" h. **$600**

Planter, h.p. w/roses, underglaze D&Co. factory mark 3, 14" h.. . . . . **$2,000**

Planter, h.p. w/roses, underglaze D&Co. factory mark 3, 14" h.. . . . . **$2,000**

Planter, h.p. w/ roses, underglaze D&Co. factory mark 3, overglaze Pickard decorating studio mark, 9" h. **$2,500**

Planter, footed w/reticulated edge, underglaze T&V factory mark 7, 9" h. **$1,500**

Planter, unusual shape, underglaze D&Co. factory mark 3, 9" l., 7" h. **$600**

Planter, unique blank w/ small handles, underglaze D&Co. factory mark 3, 12-1/2" l., 8" h.
. . . . **$2,000**

Planter, w/blown out edging, underglaze D&Co. factory mark 3, 9-1/2" l., 9" h. **$2,000**

Planter, underglaze D&Co., factory mark 3, overglaze D&Co., decorating mark 5, 12" l., 2" h. **$250**

Planter or pudding bowl, underglaze T&V factory mark 7, overglaze T&V decorating mark 16, 12" l., 2" h. **$250**

Planter w/feet, h.p. w/roses, artist signed "Reury," no discernible mark, 8" d., 7" h. **$650**

Chapter 28

Plaques

Plaques were specifically created to be pieces of art to hang on a wall, indicated by the factory pierced hole in the back and a wire for hanging. Plaques were not to be used as dinnerware, like the charger or chop plate that has found its way onto our walls. Unlike the Limoges painting on porcelain (which was square and usually imported as a blank and hand painted by an amateur artist), plaques are round and most were decorated in a factory studio and signed by a French factory artist. Plaques range from 8 to 32 inches in diameter.

Plaque, 13" d., h.p. in factory, artist signed "Bronsillon," Coronet factory mark 1. . . . . **$1,250**

Plaque, 13" d., h.p. in factory, artist signed "Duval," Coronet factory mark 1. . . . . **$1,250**

Plaque, 10" d., h.p. in factory, artist signed "Luc," Coronet factory mark 1. . . . . **$650**

Plaque, 13" d., h.p. in factory, artist signed "Dumanteil," no mark **$1,250**

Plaque, 13" d., h.p. in factory, artist signed "Duval," Coronet factory mark 1. . . . . **$950**

Plaque, 13" d., h.p. in factory, artist signed "Alixs" or "Alexos," underglaze Limoges France factory mark 2, overglaze Lazeyras, Rosenfeld, & Lehman decorating mark 3 . . . . **$1,250**

Plaque, 13" d., h.p. in factory by unknown artist, Straus, Lewis & Sons factory mark in brown **$1,250**

Plaque, 13" d., h.p. in factory, artist signed "J. Kim," underglaze Limoges France factory mark 2, overglaze Limoges France decorating mark 8 . . . . **$950**

Plaque, 11" d., h.p. in factory, artist signed "Duval," Coronet factory mark 1. . . . . **$650**

Plaque, 11" d., h.p. in factory, artist signed "Golis" or "Golse," Coronet factory mark 1 . . . . **$650**

Plaque, 14" d., h.p. w/gold gild, no markings, attributed to Limoges factory **$1,200**

Plaque, 12" d., h.p. in factory, artist signed "Ramon," overglaze Borgfeldt mark 1. . . . . **$1,500**

Plaque, 16" d., h.p. in factory, artist signed "A. Bronssillon," overglaze Borgfeldt decorating mark 1
. . . . **$2,000**

Plaque, 11" d., h.p. in factory, artist signed "A. Bronssillon," overglaze Borgfeldt decorating mark 1
. . . . **$1,500**

Plaque, 16" d., h.p. in factory, artist signed "A. Bronssillon," overglaze Borgfeldt decorating mark 1
. . . . **$2,000**

Plaque, 16" d., h.p. in factory, artist signed "A. Bronssillon," overglaze Borgfeldt decorating mark 1
. . . . **$2,000**

Plaque, 16" d., h.p. in factory, artist signed "A. Bronssillon," overglaze Borgfeldt decorating mark 1
. . . . **$2,000**

Plaque, 14" d., h.p. in factory, artist signed "A. Bronssillon," overglaze Borgfeldt decorating mark 1
. . . . **$2,000**

Plaque, 16" d., h.p. in factory, artist signed "Duval," overglaze Borgfeldt decorating mark 1 . . . . **$1,500**

Plaque, 16" d., h.p. in factory, artist signed "Duval," overglaze Borgfeldt decorating mark 1 . . . . **$1,500**

Plaque, 14" d., h.p. in factory, artist signed "A. Bronssillon," overglaze Borgfeldt decorating mark 1 . . . . **$2,000**

Plaque, 13-1/2" d., h.p. in factory, artist signed "J. Soustre," overglaze studio Lazeyras, Rosenfeld & Lehman factory mark 3 . . . . **$1,500**

Plaque, 13-1/2" d., h.p. in factory, artist signed "J. Soustre," overglaze studio Lazeyras, Rosenfeld & Lehman factory mark 3 . . . . **$1,500**

Plaque, 14" d., h.p. in factory, underglaze Limoges France factory mark 2, Lewis Straus & Sons, overglaze decorating & import mark. **$600**

Plaque, 14" d., h.p. in factory, artist signed "A. Bronssillon," overglaze Borgfeldt decorating mark 1
. . . . **$2,000**

Plaque, 12-3/4" d., h.p. in factory, artist signed "Dubois," cobalt blue, underglaze Guerin factory mark 3, overglaze Guerin decorating mark 4 . . . . **$2,500**

Plaque, 16" d., h.p. in factory, artist signed "Dubois," underglaze Sazerat, L., mark 1, overglaze Lewis Straus & Sons exporting mark 1 . . . . **$3,500**

Plaque, 12" d., underglaze Guerin factory mark 2
. . . . **$1,200**

Plaque, 12" d., underglaze LDB&C factory mark 1, overglaze Flambeau China decorating mark 4 . . **$1,200**

Plaque, 14" d., h.p. in factory, artist signed "Duval," underglaze LDB&C factory mark 1, overglaze Flambeau China decorating mark 4 . . . . **$2,000**

Plaque, 17" d., h.p. in factory by "E. Furlaud" & "D'APRE'S Gerard," back states "L'Amour et Psyche," no factory marks, attributed to Limoges **$2,500**

Plaque, 14", h.p. in factory, artist signed "Baumy," underglaze Lazeyras, Rosenfeld & Lehman factory mark 3, overglaze in red "Dans les Reves D'Apres CH. Lenoir Hand Painted" **$2,000**

Plaque, 14", h.p. in factory, artist signed "Dubois," factory Lazeyras, Rosenfeld & Lehman mark 2 in red **$1,500**

Plaque, 11", h.p. in factory, artist signed "Cibot," underglaze Lazeyras, Rosenfeld & Lehman mark 3 .... **$1,800**

Plaque, 13" d., underglaze Coiffe factory mark 3 . **$700**

Plaque, 14" d., h.p. by amateur artist "Martha Ross after Ellen Welby," underglaze Haviland factory mark D **$475**

Plaque, 13"
d., under-
glaze Coiffe
factory mark
3. . . . .**$700**

Plaque, 13" d., underglaze Coiffe factory mark 3
. . . . **$300**

Plaque, 13"
d., under-
glaze Coiffe
factory mark
3. . . . .**$700**

Plaque, 14" d., underglaze Haviland factory mark H
. . . . **$700**

Plaque, 13-1/2" d., artist signed "Rory," underglaze
Flambeau China mark 2 . . . . **$700**

Plaque, 13-1/2" d., artist signed "Albert," underglaze
Flambeau China mark 2 . . . . **$700**

Plaque, 11-1/2" d., underglaze Lazeyras, Rosenfeld & Lehman factory mark 3 . . . . **$700**

Plaque, 13-1/2" d., h.p. w/unique subject matter pug dog & tabby cat, factory artist signed "Bazanan," over the glaze "Hand Painted," Lazeyras, Rosenfeld, Lehman mark 6 . . . . **$2,500**

Plaque, 10-1/2" d., h.p. in factory, artist signed "LePic," underglaze Borgfeldt factory mark 1, overglaze Coronet decorating mark 1 . . . . **$450**

Plaque, 10-1/2" d., h.p. in factory, artist signed "LePic," underglaze Borgfeldt mark 1, overglaze Coronet decorating mark 1 . . . . . . **$450**

Plaque, 13" d., h.p. in factory, artist signed "Dubois," underglaze Borgfeldt mark 1, overglaze Coronet decorating mark 1 . . . . **$1,500**

Plaque, 12-1/2" d., h.p. in factory, artist signed "J. Soustre," overglaze studio Lazeyras, Rosenfeld & Lehman factory mark 3 . . . . **$1,500**

Chapter 29

Punch Bowls

During the Victorian Era, a Limoges punch bowl would have been stationed on a sideboard and used for serving an alcoholic or non-alcoholic punch. Sometimes the host would serve both, and this accounts for matching punch bowls. The Limoges factories produced some beautiful punch bowls, some with bases and scalloped edges, and as large as 26 inches in diameter. Bowls were accompanied by matching bases, under plates or trays, and cups or mugs. Due to the fragility of porcelain, many of the cups, mugs, and bases have not survived, or have been separated from their original bowls. In addition, punch bowls were less expensive if purchased as blanks and then hand painted by the amateur artist. The artist could choose her bowl and style of cup, and decide if she wanted a base or tray to place her punch bowl on. This fact accounts for many bowls with bases, cups, and trays (obviously hand painted as part of a set), yet each produced in a different factory.

Punch bowl, w/six cups & matching tray, 15-1/2" d., 7" h., h.p. in factory, all pieces artist signed "B. Aubin," underglaze T&V factory mark 7, overglaze L.R.L. decorating mark 3 . . . . **Set $7,000**

Unique punch bowl w/base & 12 cups, 14" d., 10" h., h.p. in American decorating studio w/burnished & etched gold, underglaze D&Co. factory mark 3, overglaze "White's Art Company Hand Painted" decorating studio mark. . . . .**Set $6,000**

Punch bowl w/base & six cups, 14" d., 9" h., h.p. w/roses & burnished gold inside & out, underglaze T&V factory mark 8 . . . .**Set $3,500**

Punch bowl w/base, matching tray & four cups, 14" d., 9" h., h.p. w/cherubs, garlands of grapes & heavy burnished gold inside & out, underglaze T&V factory mark 8 . . . .**Set $6,500**

Punch bowl w/base, 14" d., 9" h., h.p. & signed by factory artist "Rory," w/roses & burnished gold inside & out, underglaze T&V factory mark 8, overglaze T&V factory mark 16b **$5,500**

Punch bowl w/base, 16" d., 9" h., h.p. & signed by factory artist "Roby," w/roses & burnished gold inside & out, underglaze T&V factory mark 8, overglaze T&V factory mark 16b . . . .**Set $6,500**

Punch bowl w/base, 14" d., 9" h., h.p. w/roses & burnished gold inside & out, underglaze T&V factory mark 8 . . . . **$3,500**

Punch bowl w/base, 14" d., 9" h., h.p. w/roses & burnished gold inside & out, underglaze T&V factory mark 8 . . . . **$3,500**

Punch bowl w/base, 14" d., 9" h., h.p. w/roses inside & out, underglaze J.P.L. factory mark 5 . . . . **$4,000**

Punch bowl w/base, 14" d., 9" h., h.p. w/roses inside & out, heavy burnished gold, underglaze J.P.L. factory mark 5 . . . . **$4,500**

Punch bowl w/base, 14" d., 9" h., h.p. w/dark grapes inside & out, underglaze T&V factory mark 8 . . **$2,500**

Punch bowl w/base, 14" d., 9" h., h.p. w/grapes inside & out, underglaze T&V factory mark 8 . . . . . . **$1,500**

Mammoth punch bowl on legs, 26" d., 13" h., h.p. w/roses, detail scrollwork inside, underglaze J.P.L. factory mark 5 . . . . **$7,500**

Punch bowl w/base, 14" d., 9" h., h.p. w/grapes inside & out, artist signed "H. Schlehuber," underglaze T&V factory mark 8 . . . . **$2,500**

Punch bowl w/base, 14" d., 10" h., artist signed & dated "L. Vance Phillips 1906," h.p. w/detailed fairies inside & heavy gold & enameling outside, underglaze T&V factory mark 7 . . . . **$3,500**

Punch bowl, 14" d., 9-1/2" h., h.p. in factory, artist signed "Pierre," underglaze Plainemaison factory mark 1, overglaze Blakeman & Henderson decorating mark 1 . . . . **$2,000**

Punch bowl, 14" d., 9-1/2" h., raised gold paste, h.p. in factory, artist signed "Pierre," underglaze Plainemaison factory mark 1, overglaze Blakeman & Henderson decorating mark 1 . . . . **$3,500**

Punch bowl, 14" d., 6" h., h.p. by amateur artist, heavy gold & raised gold enameling, underglaze T&V factory mark 7 . . . . **$3,000**

Punch bowl, 18" d., 9" h., h.p. in factory, underglaze J.P.L. factory mark 5, overglaze J.P.L. decorating mark 7 . . . . **$2,500**

Punch bowl, 14" d., 6" h., h.p. by amateur artist, burnished gold, underglaze T&V factory mark 7 . . . . **$1,500**

Punch bowl, 14" d., 6" h., h.p. by amateur artist, gold & raised gold enameling, no marks, attributed to Limoges **$900**

Punch bowl, 10" d., 5" h., underglaze T&V factory mark 8, overglaze Pickard decorating studio mark **$2,000**

Punch bowl, 10" d., 5" h., underglaze T&V factory mark 8, overglaze Pickard decorating studio mark w/ paper import sticker **$2,500**

Punch bowl, 10" d., 5" h., h.p. by amateur artist, underglaze T&V factory mark 8 . . . . **$900**

Punch bowl w/handles, artist signed "Yvonne Beary Klapec," underglaze T&V factory mark 8a $1,500

Punch bowl, 10" d., 5" h., h.p. by amateur artist & signed "N.E. Millard," underglaze T&V factory mark 8
. . . . $1,200

Punch bowl on four gold feet, 14" d., 7" h., w/ matching tray, h.p. by amateur artist, underglaze T&V factory mark 7 . . . . $4,000

Matching tray, h.p. w/raised gold-paste scroll, underglaze T&V factory mark 7, 18" d $2,000

Punch bowl on four gold feet, 14" d., 7" h., underglaze T&V factory mark 7 . . . . $2,000

Punch bowl on four gold feet, 14" d., 7" h., scalloped edge, underglaze T&V factory mark 7 . . . . $3,000

Punch bowl on base, 9" d., 12" h., underglaze T&V factory mark 7 . . . . **$2,000**

Punch bowl on base, 9" d., 12" h., scalloped edge, underglaze T&V factory mark 7 . . . . **$2,500**

Punch bowl on tray, 12" d., 6" h., h.p. w/grapes & heavy burnished gold, underglaze T&V factory mark 7 . . . .**Set $2,000**

Punch bowl on base w/matching tray, 14" d., 9-1/2" h., h.p. w/grapes & heavy burnished gold base, underglaze T&V factory mark 7 . . . .**Set $3,000**

Punch bowl, 9" d., 6" h., h.p. w/heavy gold accents, scalloped edge, underglaze T&V factory mark 7 . . . .**$1,500**

Punch bowl, 9" d., 6" h., h.p. w/burnished edge, underglaze T&V factory mark 7 . . . . **$900**

Chapter 30

Tableware

Many items were created in the factories to accompany the dinnerware sets being produced and imported to the United States from the 1880s until World War II. These items included practical items like salt and pepper shakers, candlesticks, baskets, and nut dishes, as well as sublime pieces such as hand-painted table crumb sweepers. Keep in mind that the major production period for Limoges was in the middle of the Victorian Era. Ostentation and embellishment was a way of life, and an everyday item could be hand painted and become a thing of beauty.

Basket/bowl, 6" d., 2-1/2" h., h.p. & signed by factory artist "Pierre," underglaze Limoges France mark 2, overglaze Blakeman & Henderson decorating mark 3
. . . . **$350**

Basket, 6" w., 4" h., h.p., underglaze T&V factory mark 5. . . . . **$250**

Basket, 4" d., 4" h., h.p., underglaze T&V factory mark 5. . . . . **$100**

Basket, 4" d., 4" h., underglaze factory mark overglaze factory mark. **$70**

Basket, 12" w., 3" h., underglaze Coiffe factory mark 3
. . . . **$450**

Compote, 6" d., 4" h., underglaze T&V factory mark 5b. **$100**

Compote, 9" d., 7" h., underglaze W.G.&Co., factory mark 2 . . . . **$200**

Compote, 9" d., 7" h., h.p. & signed by amateur artist "Andrew," underglaze Haviland factory mark H **$900**

Candlesticks, h.p. w/burnished gold, underglaze W.G.&Co. factory mark 3, 8" h. . . . .**Pair $400**

Candlesticks, h.p. w/flowers & burnished gold, underglaze T&V factory mark 7, 16" h. . . . .**Pair $800**

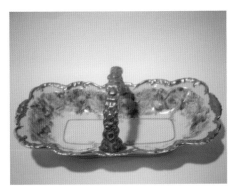

Nappy, h.p., underglaze J.P.L. factory mark 5. . . **$195**

Nappy w/basket handle, decorated using the mixtion technique, underglaze J.P.L., Pouyat factory mark 5, overglaze Pouyat decorating mark 9 . . . . **$200**

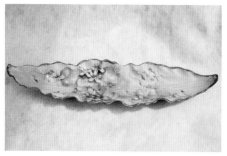

Nappy, h.p. w/violets, underglaze J.P.L. factory mark 5
. . . . **$395**

Nappy, h.p. w/berries & artist signed "Andrew," underglaze J.P.L. factory mark 5 . . . . **$295**

Nut dishes, underglaze T&V factory mark 7
. . . . **Set of 12 $100**

Salt cellars w/master salt, underglaze T&V factory mark 7 . . . . **Set $150**

Salt & pepper shaker, h.p. w/peacocks, no mark attributed to Limoges . . . . **Pair $100**

Powdered sugar shaker, h.p. w/flowers, underglaze AK factory mark 7. . . . . **$125**

Powdered sugar shaker, h.p., outlined in black, blown out blank, no discernible mark, attributed to Limoges, 4-1/2" h. $175

Powdered sugar shaker, h.p. w/flowers, underglaze AK factory mark 7. . . . . $125

Dust pan, h.p. & amateur artist signed "McFeeley," underglaze T&V factory mark 7. . . . . $600

Loving cup w/three handles, underglaze J.P.L. Pouyat factory mark 5, 6" h. $250

Loving cup w/three handles, underglaze J.P.L., Pouyat factory mark 5, 7-1/2" h. $350

Chalice, h.p. w/burnished & raised gold paste, underglaze T&V factory mark 7, 10" h. $800

Chalice, h.p. w/Victorian lady, artist signed "S.N. Fanar," underglaze T&V factory mark 7, 10" h. **$800**

Chalice, h.p. w/dark roses, underglaze T&V factory mark 7, 10" h. **$600**

Nappy, w/small handle decorated using the mixtion technique, underglaze J.P.L., Pouyat factory mark 5 . . . . **$100**

Nappy, w/handle h.p. w/plums, underglaze AK factory mark 7 . . . . **$100**

Candlesticks, h.p. w/berries & burnished gold, underglaze B&C factory mark 2, 8" h. . . . . . **Pair $400**

(Left) Tankard, h.p. w/cherries, dragon handle, underglaze T&V factory mark 7, signed Atnock, 10" h., ... **$900**

(Right) Condensed milk holder, h.p. w/cherries, underglaze D&C factory mark 3, 4" h. **$250**

Condensed milk holder w/ underplate, h.p. w/currants, underglaze D&C factory mark 3, 4" h. **$250**

Condensed milk holder w/ underplate, underglaze Limoges France factory mark 6, 4" h.. **$250**

Condensed milk holder w/ underplate, h.p. w/blackberries, underglaze D&C factory mark 3, 4" h. **$350**

Chapter 31

Tankards

A tankard with matching mugs made a lovely presentation when serving lemonade, wine, or ale at a Victorian event. Tankards are cylindrical in shape, have a handle, and range from 10 to 18 inches tall. They are not bulbous like a cider pitcher or as ornate as a ewer. Tankard sets decorated in the factory included matching mugs and sometimes a tray, and all had the same factory marks. Tankard sets decorated by the amateur artist are unique. The artist could select any tankard, mug, or tray blank available on the market. As a result, there are many amateur decorated tankard sets as unique as the individual who hand painted them. Due to the common practice of the artist selecting pieces individually, sets may include porcelain pieces other than Limoges.

Tankard, h.p. w/roses & gold handle, underglaze J.P.L. factory mark 5, 15" h. **$2,000**

Tankard, h.p. w/roses, underglaze J.P.L. factory mark 5, 14-1/2" h. **$1,000**

Tankard, h.p. w/child holding a pug, underglaze J.P.L. factory mark 5, 14-1/2" h. **$2,000**

Tankard, h.p. in factory & artist signed (illegible) w/roses & gold handle, underglaze T&V factory mark 7, overglaze T&V decorating mark 16, 15" h. $2,000

Tankard, h.p. in factory & artist signed "Roby," w/roses & gold handle, underglaze T&V factory mark 8, overglaze T&V decorating mark 16, 13" h. $900

Tankard, h.p. in factory & artist signed (illegible), w/roses & gold handle, underglaze T&V factory mark 7, overglaze T&V decorating mark 16, 14-1/2" h. $1,200

Tankard, h.p. w/lady & cherubs, underglaze D & C factory mark 3, 13" h.

. . $1,500

Tankard, h.p. in factory & artist signed "Bronsillon," w/yellow roses & gold handle, underglaze T&V factory mark 7, overglaze T&V decorating mark 16, 14-1/2" h. $900

Tankard, h.p. w/mums & raised gold-paste decoration, underglaze T&V factory mark 7, 13" h. . . . $300

Tankard, h.p. w/grapes, underglaze J.P.L. factory mark 5, 15" h. . . $900

Tankard, h.p. w/grapes, underglaze W.G.&Co., Guerin factory mark 2, 14" h.. . . . . $400

Tankard, h.p. w/roses, artist signed, underglaze J.P.L. factory mark 5, 14-1/2" h. $1,500

Tankard, h.p. w/grapes, underglaze
J.P.L. factory mark 3, 15" h. . .**$800**

Tankard **mug**, h.p. w/berries,
underglaze W.G.&Co., Guerin
factory mark 2, 5-1/2" h. **$90**

Tankard **mug**, h.p. w/berries,
underglaze A.K. factory mark 3, 4"
h. **$100**

Tankard **mug**, h.p. w/berries,
underglaze Guerin factory mark 3,
6" h. **$90**

(Left) Tankard, h.p. w/currants,
underglaze A.K. factory mark 7, 13"
h. **$800**
(Right) Tankard, h.p. w/currants,
gold leaf handle, underglaze T&V
factory mark 7, 16" h. **$900**

Tankard, h.p. w/blackberries,
underglaze Guerin factory mark 3,
14" h. **$900**

Tankard, h.p. w/berries, gold-leaf
handle, underglaze T&V factory
mark 7, 16" h. **$900**

(Left) Tankard, h.p. w/berries,
underglaze J.P.L. factory mark 5, 14"
h. **$1,200**
(Right) Condensed milk holder,
h.p. w/berries, underglaze T&V
mark 7, 4" h. **$350**

Tankard, h.p. w/cherries, underglaze
J.P.L. factory mark 5, 14" h. . .**$800**

Tankards 199

Chapter 32

Teapots

Teapots come in a large range of sizes and shapes, from the single-cup pot, up to an eight-cup pot. Teapots are squattier than chocolate and coffee pots, with the shape allowing for the expansion of the tea leaves. Another distinct characteristic of a teapot is its spout. Tea sets normally came with a pot, creamer and sugar, and sometimes a cake plate, dessert plates, and matching cups and saucers. Tea sets were not included as part of a dinnerware set, but were purchased separately.

Tea set: pot, sugar bowl, creamer & tray, h.p. w/violets, underglaze J.P.L. factory mark 5 . . . . **Set $2,000**

Tea set: pot, sugar bowl, creamer & tray, h.p. & artist signed "ATK" w/violets, underglaze J.P.L. factory mark 5 . . . . **Set $800**

Tea set: pot, sugar bowl & creamer, h.p. (most Haviland was decorated using the transferware method), w/artist initials "M. M. DYE 1901," Theo Haviland Limoges France, mark L, 1893 . . . . **Set $750**

Tea set: pot, sugar bowl, creamer & tray, h.p. w/roses, artist signed & dated "C. Wynn 1901," underglaze T&V factory mark 6 . . . . **Set $1,000**

Tea set: pot, sugar bowl & creamer, underglaze Limoges France factory mark 1 . . . . **Set $600**

Tea set: pot, sugar bowl, creamer, & tray, h.p. w/roses & heavy burnished gold scrollwork, underglaze J.P.L. factory mark 5 . . . . **Set $2,000**

Tea set: pot, sugar bowl & creamer, h.p. w/roses & cherubs, artist signed & dated "MY 1904," underglaze J.P.L. factory mark 5 . . . . **Set $2,000**

Tea set: pot, sugar bowl, creamer & tray, h.p. w/roses, underglaze AK factory mark 7 . . . . **Set $1,000**

Tea set: pot, sugar bowl, creamer & tray, h.p. light green w/raised enamel scrolled paste, underglaze T&V factory mark 4 . . . .**Set $1,500**

Tea set: pot, sugar bowl & creamer, h.p. w/roses, underglaze D&Co. factory mark 3 . . . .**Set $1,500**

Teapot, h.p. w/roses & gold scroll & spider web, underglaze T&V factory mark 7 . . . . **$850**

Tea set: pot, sugar bowl & creamer, h.p. w/roses, underglaze W.G.&Co. factory mark 2 . . . . .**Set $1,500**

Tea set: pot, sugar, creamer, decorated w/ decal, underglaze J.P.L. factory mark 5, overglaze J.P.L. decorating mark 8 . . . . **Set $250**

Tea set: pot, sugar, creamer, waste bowl, cake plate, four cups & saucers, & four berry bowls, decorated in Dresden style w/gold, marked "Elite L France," Bawo & Dotter mark 5, after 1900. . . . . **Set $2,000**

Teapot, h.p. on inside, artist initials "KLR 1890," AK Klingenberg mark 3, 1880s-1890 . . . . **$900**

Teapot, h.p. roses & raised gold-enamel scrolling, Elite L France, Bawo & Dotter mark 5, after 1900 . . . . . **$495**

Teapot, h.p. w/roses & bows, J.P.L. France, Pouyat mark 5, 1891-1932, 4" h. **$395**

Teapot, h.p. w/roses & gold scroll & spider web, underglaze T&V factory mark 7. . . . . **$850**

Tea set: pot, sugar, creamer, two cups & saucers, underglaze Mavaleix factory mark 1. . . . . **Set $1,500**

Tea set: pot, sugar, creamer, underglaze & overglaze B&C factory mark. . . . . **Set $1,200**

Tea set: pot, sugar, creamer, all artist signed "Klineberg," underglaze J.P.L. factory mark 5 . . . **Set $1,500**

Tea set: pot, sugar, creamer, all artist signed "Rancon," underglaze Borgfeldt factory mark 1, overglaze Limoges France decorating mark 2
................Set $2,500

Tea strainer w/underliner, underglaze T&V factory mark 5a $495

Tea strainer w/underliner, underglaze T&V factory mark 7 ....$495

Large sugar bowl, h.p. in factory w/roses, underglaze Bawo & Dotter factory mark 5, overglaze Elite France mark 1 ....$150

Tea caddy, 3-1/4 x 3-1/2", 2-1/4" h., underglaze Guerin factory mark 2 ....$100

Creamer & sugar, underglaze Haviland factory mark I .... Set $100

Creamer & sugar, underglaze Guerin factory mark 3 .... Set $100

Chapter 33

Trays

Trays were placed under dresser sets, punch bowls, tankards, cider pitchers, teapots, coffee pots, and chocolate pots. Trays can run from a mere 3-inch long pin tray to more than 24 inches for some ornate service platters and trays. Most trays were part of a set, but if found individually, are beautiful pieces of art.

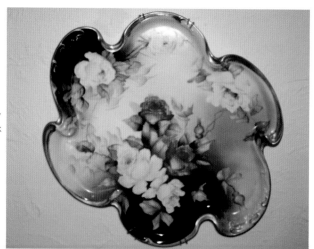

Tray, h.p. & artist signed "E. Miler," underglaze W.G.&Co., factory mark 3, 18" d............... **$2,000**

Tray, h.p. & artist signed "E.I. Richardson," underglaze Limoges France factory mark 1, 14" w. **$1,200**

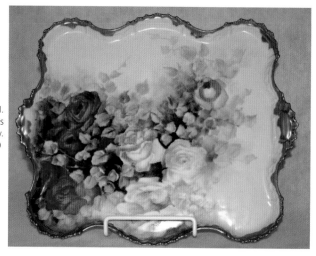

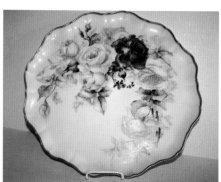

Tray, h.p., underglaze W.G.&Co., factory mark 3, 18" d................................ **$1,200**

Tray, h.p. w/gold gilt, underglaze T&V factory mark 7, 16" d................................ **$1,200**

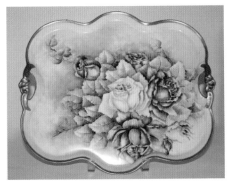

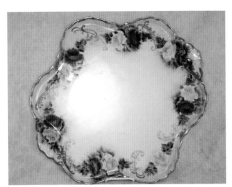

Tray w/handles, h.p., underglaze T&V factory mark 7, 14" d.. . . . .**$800**

Tray w/scalloped edges, h.p., underglaze T&V factory mark 7, 24" d.. . . . .**$1,200**

Tray, h.p., underglaze GDA factory mark 1, 16" d. **$800**

Tray, h.p., underglaze T&V factory mark 7, 18" d. **$1,200**

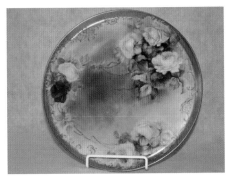

Tray, h.p., underglaze GDA factory mark 1, 16" d. **$800**

Tray, h.p., underglaze T&V factory mark 5a, 14" d. **$600**

Tray, h.p., underglaze J.P.L. factory mark 5, 14" w.
.... **$800**

Tray, h.p., underglaze T&V factory mark 7, 14" d.
.... **$500**

Tray, h.p., underglaze J.P.L. factory mark 5, 12" d.
.... **$300**

Tray, h.p., underglaze D&Co., factory mark 3, 12" d.
.... **$400**

Ice cream tray, h.p. in factory w/roses, artist signed "Roby," underglaze T&V factory mark 5, overglaze T&V factory mark 13, 9-1/2" w., 16" l.............. **$500**

Ice cream tray, h.p. by amateur artist "Whiley," underglaze T&V factory mark 8, 9-1/2" w., 16" l.
.... **$500**

Ice cream tray, h.p. by amateur artist "Driscoll," underglaze T&V factory mark 8, 9-1/2" w., 16" l. **$400**

Ice cream tray, underglaze T&V factory mark 8, 9-1/2" w., 16" l. **$400**

Dresser tray, h.p. in factory w/roses, artist signed "A. Lajus," underglaze T&V factory mark 5, overglaze T&V factory mark 13, 11" w. **$500**

Dresser tray, h.p. w/soft roses, underglaze T&V factory mark 5, 11" d. **$250**

Dresser tray, h.p. w/raised gold paste & soft roses, underglaze T&V factory mark 5, 8" w., 12" l. **$350**

Pin tray w/handles, W.G.&Co. factory mark 3, 3" w., 4" l. **$50**

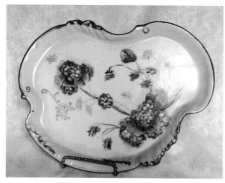

Dresser tray, h.p. w/violets, W.G.&Co. factory mark 3, 12" d.. . . . .**$250**

Pin tray, part of dresser set, no factory mark, 3" w., 4" l.. . . . .**$30**

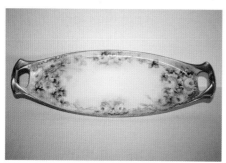

Tray, h.p. w/raised gold paste & enameling, artist signed & dated "Emily Reid 1906," underglaze W.G.&Co. factory mark 3, 5-1/2" w., 13" l.. . . . .**$500**

Tray w/split handle, h.p., underglaze W.G.&Co. factory mark 3, 4" w., 12" h.. . . . .**$395**

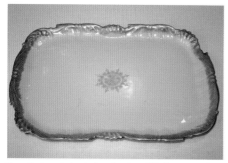

Tray, factory decorated, underglaze T&V factory mark 7, overglaze T&V factory mark 14, 8" w., 12-1/2" l.. **$150**

Tray, h.p., amateur artist "M.S.T.," underglaze J.P.L. factory mark 5, 6" w., 11" l.. . . . .**$250**

Tray, h.p., w/scene from Othello, heavy ornate gold gilt raised paint & enameling, underglaze T&V factory mark 8, 18" d..**$3,000**

Dresser tray, h.p. by amateur, underglaze J.P.L. factory mark 5, 8" w., 11" l. **$300**

Tray w/reticulated edge, h.p. w/lovers kissing, underglaze J.P.L. factory mark 5, 12" w., 12" l..........**$1,200**

Tray, h.p. romantic scene w/raised gold scroll, underglaze T&V factory mark 7, 12-1/2" w., 16" l. . **$1,500**

Dresser tray, h.p. w/two ladies, no mark, blank attributed to Limoges, 12" w., 14" l. **$400**

Dresser tray, h.p. in factory w/romantic scene, artist signed "Petit," underglaze T&V factory mark 7, 16" w., 16" l. **$900**

Serving tray, h.p. w/Currier & Ives winter scene, underglaze Haviland factory mark F., 9" w., 14" l. **$1,200**

Tray w/handles, h.p. w/dark grapes, underglaze J.P.L. factory mark 5, 12" d. **$400**

Tray, h.p. w/heavy burnished gold, underglaze J.P.L. factory mark 5, 14" w., 14" l. **$800**

Tray, under tray for punch bowl, underglaze J.P.L. factory mark 5, 13" w., 16" l. **$800**

Tray, h.p. w/etched burnished gold & rose center, underglaze Vignaud Freres factory mark 1, 12-1/2" w., 16-1/2" l. **$500**

Tray, w/tiny handle, underglaze T&V factory mark 7, 4" w., 9" l. **$250**

Serving tray, h.p. & artist signed & dated "Squire '95" (1895), no discernible factory marks, 19" w., 14" l. **$800**

Tray, h.p., underglaze Lanternier factory mark 4, 12" d. **$250**

Chapter 34

Vases

Vases exhibit the most diverse blanks or shapes of any Limoges produced. They can be curvaceous, cylindrical, or bulbous, tall or short, and with handles or without. They vary from very short and squat to so tall that several pieces may be bolted together. Some have necks wide enough to house two dozen roses; others have thin necks that can fit only the stem of a single flower. Many of these vases were decorated in a Limoges decorating factory, while others were decorated by amateur artists.

Vase, 9-1/2" h., underglaze J.P.L., Pouyat factory mark 5. . . . . **$900**

Vase, 9-1/2" h., underglaze J.P.L., Pouyat factory mark 5. . . . . **$900**

Vase, 12" h., underglaze J.P.L., Pouyat factory mark 7. . . . . . **$350**

Vase, 11-1/2" h., underglaze B&Co., Bernardaud factory mark 1 . . **$900**

Vase, 16" h., h.p. w/heavy raised gold paste & gold handles, blank unmarked but attributed to Limoges **$2,500**

Vase, 16" h., h.p. w/heavy raised gold paste & gold handles, blank unmarked but attributed to Limoges **$2,500**

Vase, 9-1/2" h., serpent-shaped handles, underglaze J.P.L. factory mark 5 . . . . **$800**

Vase, 15" h., h.p. w/roses & burnished gold, underglaze J.P.L factory mark 5 . . . . **$2,000**

 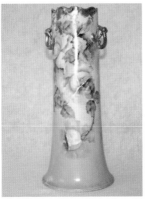 

Vase, 16" h., h.p. w/heavy raised gold paste & gold handles, blank unmarked but attributed to Limoges **$500**

Vase, 15" h., h.p. w/raised gold paste, underglaze W.G.&Co., factory mark 3 . . . . **$1,000**

Vase, 16" h., h.p. w/heavy raised gold paste & gold handles, blank unmarked but attributed to Limoges **$1,000**

Vase, 8-1/2" h., w/handles, underglaze J.P.L. factory mark 5 . . . . **$300**

Vase, 12-1/2" h., underglaze Latrille Freres factory mark 1 . . . . . **$1,000**

Vase, 18" h., underglaze T&V, factory mark 4b **$2,500**

Vase, palace urn blank, 20" h., h.p. w/gold wear on neck, underglaze T&V, factory mark 4b **$3,000**

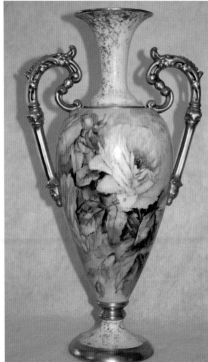

Vase, 9" h., w/split gold handles & raised enamel, underglaze J.P.L. factory mark 5 . . . . **$700**

Vase, 15" h., underglaze W.G.&Co., factory mark 3 . . . . **$900**

Vase, 14" h., w/gold gilded lion handles, h.p. & artist signed "Mrs. CW Lamson, Erie, PA, March 16, 1905," underglaze D&Co., factory mark 3 . . . . **$2,500**

Vase, 6" h., underglaze J.P.L. factory mark 5, overglaze "Hand Painted" **$450**

Vase on legs, 14-1/2" h., h.p., underglaze W.G.&Co., factory mark 3. **$1,000**

Vase on legs, 14-1/2" h., h.p., underglaze W.G.&Co., factory mark 3. **$1,000**

Vase on legs, 14" h., h.p. ornate blank w/heavy gold, underglaze T&V, factory mark 7 . . . . . . **$1,500**

Vase on base (front, left; back, right), 12-1/2" h., underglaze J.P.L. factory mark 3 . . . . **$2,500**

Cachepot, 11" h., underglaze
W.G.&Co., factory mark 3. . . .**$200**

Cachepot, 11" h., underglaze mark
Bavaria, attributed to William Guerin
factory **$1,000**

Cachepot, 11" h., underglaze
W.G.&Co., factory mark 3
. . . . **$1,200**

Cachepot, 11" h., underglaze
W.G.&Co., factory mark 3. . **$1,200**

Cachepot, 11" h., underglaze
W.G.&Co., factory mark 3. . **$1,200**

Cachepot, 9" h., underglaze
W.G.&Co., factory mark 3. . . .**$900**

Cachepot, 9" h., underglaze
W.G.&Co., factory mark 3. . . .**$200**

Cachepot, 9" h., underglaze
W.G.&Co., factory mark 3. . . .**$300**

Cachepot, 11" h., underglaze
W.G.&Co., factory mark 3. . . .**$800**

Cachepot, 9" h., underglaze W.G.&Co., factory mark 3. . . .**$300**

Cachepot, 9" h., underglaze W.G.&Co., factory mark 3. . . .**$800**

Cachepot, 6" h., underglaze W.G.&Co., factory mark 3. . . .**$300**

Vase, 14" h., h.p., in standard method of painting, underglaze J.P.L. factory mark 5 . . . .**$1,500**

Vase, 14" h., h.p., burnished gold rim, underglaze T&V factory mark 7 . . . . **$1,500**

Vase, 14" h., h.p., underglaze T&V factory mark 7 . . . . **$1,500**

Vase, rose bowl, 7-1/2" h., artist initials on bottom "M.W.," underglaze J.P.L. factory mark 5, import mark L. Cooley, Boston (U.S.A.). **$500**

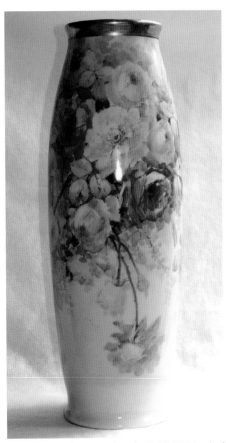

Vase, 17" h., underglaze B&C factory mark 1. . **$2,000**

Vase, 22-1/2" h., artist signed "R SCHOLZ," raised enameling over the h.p. roses, underglaze B&C factory mark 1 . . . . **$3,000**

Vase, 14" h., h.p. in Deco Style w/burnished gold, underglaze T&V factory mark 7 . . . . **$400**

Vase, 12" h., factory decorated & artist signed "F. Poujol," underglaze Décor Main Limoges France, Castel factory mark, ca. 1980s **$300**

Vase, 9" h., h.p. w/enameling, underglaze J.P.L. factory mark 5 . . . . **$450**

Vase, 17" h., underglaze T&V factory mark 7 . . .**$2,000**

Vase, 14" h., underglaze W.G.&Co., factory mark 3
. . . .**$1,200**

Vase, 14" h., h.p. by amateur artist & signed "M.D.E. Peterson," underglaze T&V factory mark 7 . . . . .**$1,500**

Vase, 12" h., h.p. by amateur artist & signed "Griffith," underglaze GDA factory mark 7 . . . .**$1,500**

Vase, 16" h., w/heavy gold rim, underglaze W.G.&Co. factory mark 3 . . . .**$1,500**

Vase, 14" h., h.p., burnished gold rim, underglaze T&V factory mark 7 . . . .**$1,500**

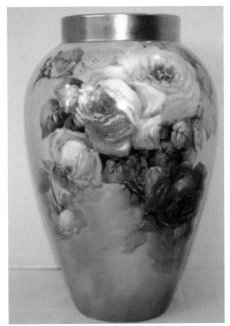

Vase, 22-1/2" h., h.p. by unknown artist, underglaze T&V factory mark 7. . . . .**$3,000**

Vase, 14" h., h.p., burnished gold rim, underglaze T&V factory mark 7 . . . .**$1,500**

Vase, 13" h., h.p. in Art Deco style, mark drilled out so piece could be made into lamp $600

Vase, 14" h., h.p., burnished gold rim, underglaze T&V factory mark 7
. . . .$1,500

Vase, 16" h., h.p. in Art Deco style, B&C mark 1 . . . . $900

Vase, 8" h., h.p. w/burnished gold & cameos w/violets, mother-of-pearl, luster of lavender color, raised gold paste, overlapping of Colonial Revival style & Art Deco style, underglaze W.G.&Co. factory mark 2 . . . . $900

Vase, squatty, 6" h., h.p., no markings. $100

Vase, 13" h., h.p. & artist signed "P. Putzki," underglaze J.P.L., Pouyat factory mark 5 . . . . **$2,000**

Urn w/cover, 22" h., h.p. & enameling, underglaze J.P.L. factory mark 5 . . . . **$2,500**

Vase, squatty, 9" d., 6" h., underglaze T&V factory mark 7. . . . .**$800**

Vase, squatty, 9" d., 6" h., underglaze T&V factory mark 7. . . . .**$800**

Vase, squatty, 14" d., 8" h., h.p. & artist signed "Vera Gray," underglaze T&V factory mark 7 . . . . **$3,000**

Vase, squatty, 9" d., 6" h., underglaze T&V factory mark 7. . . . .**$200**

Vases 231

Vase, 16" h.p., w/etched gold, artist signed "Laura H. Haste 1922," underglaze B&C factory mark 1.. **$2,500**

Vase, 22" h., bolted base, h.p. w/burnished gold & raised enameling, artist signed "Geo. T. Porter," underglaze W.G.&Co., factory mark 2. . . . . **$3,000**

Vase, 16" h., h.p. w/peacock, underglaze T&V factory mark 7 . . . . **$1,500**

Vase, 11" h., h.p. in factory & artist signed "Dubois," underglaze W.G.&Co., factory mark 2, overglaze W.G.&Co., decorating mark 4. . . . . **$2,500**

Vase, 15" h., h.p. in Dresden factory, w/portrait of a woman, heavy raised gold paste, overglaze "Dresden" in blue w/crown, overglaze gold shield on top of an underglaze W.G.&Co. factory mark 2 . . . .**$7,500**

Vase, 11" h., h.p. w/ scene & heavy raised enamel, artist signed "Minneh Freeoff 1895," underglaze J.P.L. factory mark 5 . . . . **$1,500**

Vase, 13" h., underglaze Latrille Freres factory mark 1 . . . . . . **$900**

Vase w/lid, 14" h., h.p., underglaze W.G.&Co., factory mark 3 . . . **$2,500**

Vase w/lid, 16" h., underglaze J.P.L. factory mark 5 . . . .**$1,500**

Vase w/lid 16" h., h.p. w/portrait raised gold paste, underglaze J.P.L. factory mark 5 . . . .**$1,500**

Vase, 14" h., h.p. w/courting scene, underglaze Elite France factory mark 5 . . . .**$1,500**

Vase, 22" h., bolted base, h.p., underglaze W.G.&Co. factory mark 2 . . . .**$2,500**

Vase, 8" h., h.p. w/fairy, underglaze W.G.&Co. factory mark 2 . . . **$900**

Vase, 22-1/2" h., h.p. w/flowers, burnished gold handles & embellishment, unique marks impressed into the porcelain in each vase, illegible word above "Limoges" . . . . **Pair $6,500**

Umbrella stand, 18" h., h.p., no marks, attributed to Limoges factory **$2,500**

Vase, 22" h., bolted base, h.p., underglaze W.G.&Co. factory mark 2. . . . . **$3,000**

Vase, 22" h., bolted base, h.p., underglaze W.G.&Co. factory mark 2. . . . . **$3,000**

Vase, 22" h., bolted base, h.p., underglaze W.G.&Co. factory mark 2 . . . . **$3,000**

Vase, 22" h., bolted base, h.p., underglaze W.G.&Co. factory mark 2 . . . . **$3,000**

Vase, palace urn, 20" h., h.p. & signed "Guillou," underglaze T&V, factory mark 4b **$9,000**

Vase, urn, 14" h., w/original gold stopper, underglaze W.G.&Co., factory mark 2 . . . . **$1,500**

Vase, 9" d., 13" h., underglaze Bernardaud & Co., factory mark 1 . . . . **$1,500**

Vase, bud, 4" d., 14" h., h.p. w/iris, underglaze Guerin factory mark 3 . . . . **$1,000**

Vase, squat bud, 9" d., 5-1/2" h., h.p. & signed by factory artist "Leona," J.P.L., Pouyat factory mark 5 . . . . **$900**

Vase, squat bud, 9-1/2" d., 4-1/2" h., h.p. w/roses, underglaze T&V mark 7 . . . . **$1,000**

Vase, 7" d., 13" h., underglaze Bernardaud & Co., factory mark 1 . . . . **$1,500**

Vase, covered urn, 9" d., 16" h., attributed as a Limoges blank, no discernible mark **$2,000**

Vase, champagne bucket, 11" d., from handle to handle, 14" h., underglaze Guerin factory mark 2 . . . . **$2,500**

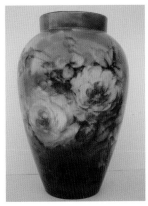

Vase, 13" h., h.p. w/roses & bluebirds, underglaze B&C factory mark 2 . . . . **$800**

Vase, 9" h., h.p. w/roses, underglaze D&C factory mark 3 . . . . **$600**

Vase, 13" h., h.p. w/roses, underglaze La Porcelaine Limousine factory mark 2 . . . . **$1,200**

Chapter 35

Wedding Ring or Wedding Band

This whiteware, hand painted with a solid gold band, is fine Limoges porcelain that was plentiful in the 19th century. Imported to the United States in mass quantities, Wedding Ring porcelain was used as everyday dinnerware by the upper middle classes. Some monogrammed their family crests or initials to individualize their sets. Families have inherited complete dinnerware sets, partial sets, and individual pieces of early Haviland and Company, and Theodore Haviland. Haviland did not mark all of its dinnerware until 1871, so it is difficult for a collector to know if a piece is actually from a set manufactured in the Haviland factory or is an inferior piece that was added to a set. Adding to the confusion is that the later-produced Limoges gold-banded porcelain of 1894 to 1931 is sometimes called Wedding Band. The old wedding ring pieces have patina gold that looks as rich and handsome as if it were wrapped in a piece of gold rope and are a bit heavier in construction than pieces produced after 1894.

Set of Wedding Ring in Streiff family home, owned for five generations.

Old Wedding Ring set: coffee pot, teapot, w/sugar bowl & creamer, marked Haviland & Company, marks F & g
. . . . **Set $300**

Old Wedding Ring coffee pot, incised H&Co, mark B $200

Old Wedding Ring single dessert set: 8" d. plate, 6" d. plate, cup & saucer, marked Haviland & Company, mark F & g . . . . Set $35

Old Wedding Ring teapot, marked Haviland & Company, marks F & g $100

Old Wedding Ring dessert set for 12: 12" d. cake plate, 8" d. dessert plate, 6" d. dessert plate, 3" d. butter pat, marked Haviland & Company, mark F & g . . . . Set $350

Old Wedding Ring plate, 8" d., marked Haviland & Company, mark F & g. $15

Old Wedding Ring cake plate, 12" d., marked Haviland & Company, mark F & g. $20

Old Wedding Ring plate, 8" d., marked Haviland & Company, mark F & g. $10

Old Wedding Ring butter pat, 3" d., marked Haviland & Company, mark F & g **$10**

Old Wedding Ring waste bowl, marked Haviland & Company, mark F & g, 6" d., 5" h.. . . . . **$45**

Old Wedding Ring cake plate, 12" d., marked Haviland & Company, mark F & g **$25**

Old Wedding Ring serving platter, 16" l., unmarked **$25**

Old Wedding Ring cup & saucer, Wedding Ring design in the bottom of the cup, marked Haviland & Company, mark F & g **$45**

Old Wedding Ring demitasse cup & saucer, marked Haviland & Company, mark F & g **$25**

Old Wedding Ring cup & saucer, marked Haviland & Company, mark F & g. **$15**

Old Wedding Ring cup & saucer, marked Haviland & Company, mark F & g. **$10**

Chapter 36
Limoges Factory Marks or Backstamps

Following is an alphabetical listing of actual photographs or an artist's rendition of Limoges factory marks. Their captions identify the factory that the mark is associated with and the date that particular mark was used. In order to be consistent, the numbering of these marks follows the same order that author Mary Frank Gaston and I have used for the last three decades. This marks section is all inclusive, but if you have a piece with a mark or marks not identified in this section, please feel free to contact me at (dlimoges@flash.net).

Ahrenfeldt, Charles J. (CA) Factory: 1859-1969

Ahrenfeldt, overglaze decorating mark in red, 1884-1893.

Ahrenfeldt, mark 1, in blue, overglaze decorating mark, after 1893.

Ahrenfeldt, mark 2, in green, underglaze factory mark, 1894-1930s.

Ahrenfeldt, mark 3, in green, underglaze factory mark, 1894-1930s.

Ahrenfeldt, mark 4, in green, underglaze factory mark, 1894-1930s.

Ahrenfeldt, mark 5, in green, underglaze factory mark, 1894-1930s.

Ahrenfeldt, mark 6, in green, underglaze factory mark, 1894-1930s.

Ahrenfeldt, mark 6a, in green, a variation of mark 6, underglaze factory mark, 1894-1930s.

Ahrenfeldt, mark 7, in green, overglaze decorating mark, 1894-1930s.

Ahrenfeldt, mark 8a, in green, red, or gold, overglaze decorating mark, 1894-1930s.

Ahrenfeldt, mark 8b, in green, overglaze decorating mark, 1894-1930s.

Ahrenfeldt, mark 9, in blue, overglaze decorating mark, after WWII until 1969.

Allaud, Fancois II (FA or AF) Factory: 1798-1876

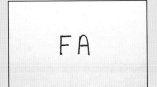

Allaud, Francois II, mark 1, overglaze decorating mark, before 1876.

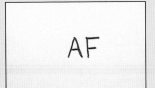

Allaud, mark 2, overglaze decorating mark, ca. 1876.

Allaud, mark 3, overglaze monogram mark, before 1876.

Aluminite Factory: 1900-1964

Ardant, Henri Factory: 1859-early 1900s

B. H. Unidentified Factory: 1920s

Aluminite, mark in green, underglaze factory mark, ca. 1920s.

Ardant, Henri, mark in green, underglaze factory mark, 1859-early 1880s.

Unidentified factory mark in green, underglaze factory mark, ca. 1920s.

Balleroy, H. Factory: 1908-late 1930s

Balleroy, H., mark 1 in green, underglaze factory mark, 1908-1930s.

Balleroy, H., mark 2 in dark green, underglaze factory mark, 1908-late 1930s.

Barny and Rigoni Factory: 1894-1906

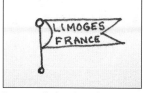

Barny and Rigoni, mark 1 in dark green, underglaze factory mark, 1894-1902.

Barny, Rigoni, and Redon, mark 2 in dark green, underglaze factory mark, 1902-1904.

Barny, Rigoni, and Langle, mark 3 in green, underglaze factory mark, 1904-1906.

Barny, Rigoni, and Langle, mark 4 in dark green, overglaze decorating mark, 1904-1906.

Bassett, George Factory: 1800s-1914

Bawo & Dotter (Elite Works) Factory: 1860s-1932

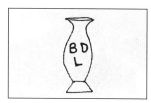

Bassett, George, mark in red, overglaze import mark, late 1800s-1914.

Bawo & Dotter, mark 1 in green, overglaze decorating mark, 1870s-1880s.

Bawo & Dotter, mark 2 in green, overglaze decorating mark, 1870s-1880s.

Bawo & Dotter, mark 2a in red, overglaze decorating mark, 1870s-1880s.

Bawo & Dotter, mark 3 in red or green, overglaze decorating mark, 1880s.

Bawo & Dotter, mark 4 in green, underglaze factory mark, 1896-1900.

Bawo & Dotter, mark 5 in green, underglaze factory mark, after 1900.

Bawo & Dotter, mark 6 in red, overglaze decorating mark, 1880s-1891.

Bawo & Dotter, mark 7 in green, underglaze factory mark, 1896-1900.

Bawo & Dotter, mark 8 in red, overglaze decorating mark, 1896-1900.

Bawo & Dotter, mark 9 in red, overglaze decorating mark, 1900-1914.

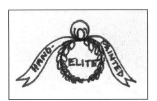

Bawo & Dotter, mark 10 in red, overglaze decorating mark, 1900-1914.

Bawo & Dotter, mark 11 in red, overglaze decorating mark, 1920-1932.

Bawo & Dotter, mark 11a in green, overglaze decorating mark, a variation of mark 11, 1920-1932.

Bawo & Dotter, mark 12 in black & brown, overglaze decorating mark, after 1920.

Limoges Factory Marks or Backstamps 245

Bernardaud & Co. (B&Co.) Factory: 1900-Present

Bernardaud & Co., mark 1 in green, underglaze factory mark, 1900-1914.

Bernardaud & Co., mark 2 in green, underglaze factory mark, 1914-1930s and after.

Bernardaud & Co., mark 3 in red, overglaze decorating mark, 1900-1930s and after.

Blakeman & Henderson (B. & H.) Factory: 1890-1900s

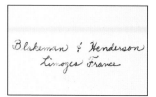

Blakeman & Henderson, mark 1, underglaze factory mark, 1920s.

Blakeman & Henderson, mark 2 in green, gray, or red circle, overglaze decorating mark, 1890s-1900s.

Blakeman & Henderson, mark 3 in green script, overglaze decorating mark, early 1900s.

Borgfeldt, George (Coronet) Factory: 1881-1976

Borgfeldt, George (Coronet), mark 1 in green or blue, overglaze decorating mark, 1906-1920.

Borgfeldt, George (Coronet), mark 2 in green, overglaze decorating mark, after 1920.

Boyer, Jean (J.B.) Factory: 1919-mid 1930s

Boyer, Jean, mark 1 in black or dark green, underglaze factory mark, 1919-mid 1930s.

Boyer, Jean, mark 2 in blue or red, overglaze decorating mark, 1919-mid 1930s.

Burley & Tyrell (BT Co.) Factory: 1900s-1912

Burley & Tyrell Company, mark in green, overglaze import mark, 1900s-1912.

C. et J. Studio: 1800s-1914

C. et J., mark in red, overglaze decorating mark, 1800s-1914.

Chabrol Freres & Poirer Factory: 1917-late 1930s

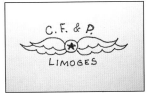

Chabrol Freres & Poirer, mark in black or dark green, underglaze factory mark, ca. 1920s.

Chapus & Ses Fils Factory: 1928-1933

Chapus & Ses Fils, mark 1 in black or dark green, underglaze factory mark, 1928-1933.

Chauffraisse, Rougerie, & Co. Factory: 1925-1930s

Chauffraisse, Rougerie, & Co., mark in black or dark green, underglaze factory mark, late 1920s.

Coiffe Factory: 1870-mid 1920s

Coiffe, mark 1 in green, underglaze factory mark, before 1890.

Coiffe, mark 2 in green, underglaze factory mark, after 1891-1914.

Coiffe, mark 3 in green, underglaze factory mark, after 1891-1914.

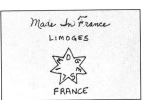

Coiffe, mark 4 in green, underglaze factory mark, 1914-1920s.

Comte D'Artois
Factory: 1930s

Comte D'Artois, mark 1 in green or red, overglaze decorating mark, late 20th century.

Creange, Henri (HC)
Factory: 1907-1914

Creange, Henri, mark 1 in green or red, underglaze factory mark, 1907-1914.

Delinieres, R. (D&Co.) Factory: 1860-1900

Delinieres, R. (D&CO.), mark 1 in green, underglaze factory mark, 1870s.

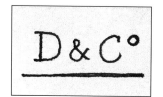

Delinieres, R. (D&CO.), mark 2 in green, underglaze factory mark, 1879-1893.

Delinieres, R. (D&CO.), mark 3 in green, underglaze factory mark, 1894-1900.

Delinieres, R. (D&CO.), mark 4 in red, overglaze decorating mark, 1881-1893.

Delinieres, R. (D&CO.), mark 5 in red, overglaze decorating mark in script form, 1894-1900.

Delinieres, R. (D&CO.), mark 6 in red, overglaze decorating mark identifying importer, 1894-1900.

Flambeau China (L. D. B. & Co.) Factory: Late 1890s-World War I

Flambeau China, mark 1 in green, underglaze factory mark, 1890s-1914.

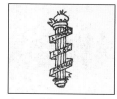

Flambeau China, mark 2 in red, overglaze decorating mark used when Flambeau was a decorating studio only, 1890s.

Flambeau China, mark 3 in green, red, or blue, overglaze decorating mark, 1890s-early 1900s.

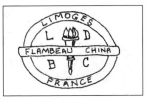

Flambeau China, mark 4 in green, overglaze decorating mark, 1890s-early 1900s.

Flambeau China, mark 4a, variation of mark 4, overglaze decorating mark, 1890s-early 1900s.

Flambeau China, mark 5 in green, overglaze decorating mark, before 1914 and after marks 2, 3, and 4.

Flambeau China, mark 6 in green, overglaze decorating mark, before 1914 and after marks 2, 3, and 4.

Fontanille and Marraud (F.M.) Factory: 1930s-Present

Fontanille and Marraud, mark 1, after 1935-present.

Fontanille and Marraud, mark 2, after 1935-present.

Fontanille and Marraud, mark 3, after 1935-present.

Fontanille and Marraud, mark 4, after 1935-present.

Francois, Andre Factory: 1919-mid 1930s

F&Co. Factory: 1920 and After

GD Factory: Early 1900s

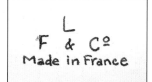

Francois, Andre, mark 1, underglaze factory mark, 1919-mid 1930s.

F&Co., mark 1, underglaze factory mark, 1920 and after.

GD, mark 1 in orange, overglaze decorating mark, early 1900s.

Gerard, Dufraisseix and Abbot (GDA) Factory: 1900-Present

Gerard, Dufraisseix and Abbot, mark 1 in green, underglaze factory mark, 1900-1941.

Gerard, Dufraisseix and Abbot, mark 2 in green, underglaze factory mark, early 1900s.

Gerard, Dufraisseix and Abbot, mark 3 in red, overglaze decorating mark, 1900-1941.

Gerard, Dufraisseix and Abbot, mark 4 in red, overglaze decorating mark, 1941-present.

Gerard, Dufraisseix, and Morel Factory: 1882-1900

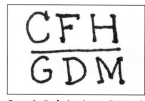

Gerard, Dufraisseix and Morel, mark 1 in green, underglaze factory mark, 1882-1890.

Gerard, Dufraisseix and Morel, mark 2 in green, underglaze factory mark, after 1891-1900.

Gerard, Dufraisseix and Morel, mark 3 in red, blue, gray, brown, or black, overglaze decorating mark, 1882-1900.

Gibus and Redon Factory: 1872-1882

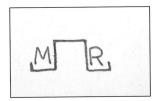

Gibus and Redon, mark 1, incised factory mark, 1872-1881.

Gibus and Redon, mark 2 in red, overglaze decorating mark, prior to 1882.

G.I.D. Factory: 1910-1930

G.I.D., mark 1 in green, underglaze factory mark, 1910-1930.

Gimbel Brothers Factory: 1930s

Gimbel Brothers, mark 1 in green or red, overglaze decorating mark, 1930s.

Giraud, A. Factory: 1920s

Giraud, A., mark 1 in dark green, underglaze factory mark, 1920s.

Granger Factory: 1922-1938

Granger, mark 1 in green, underglaze factory mark, 1922-1938.

Granger, mark 2 in green, underglaze factory mark, 1922-1938.

Granger, mark 3 in black & gold, overglaze decorating mark, 1922-1938.

Guerin, William (W.G.&Co.) Factory: 1836-1932

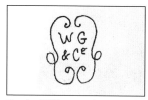

Guerin, William, mark 1 in green, underglaze factory mark, 1870s.

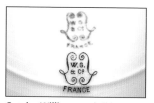

Guerin, William, mark 2 in green, underglaze factory mark, 1891-1900. (Also shown rare Guerin decorating mark in red, 1890s-1900.)

Guerin, William, mark 3 in green, underglaze factory mark, 1900-1932. (Also shown Guerin mark 4 in blue.)

Guerin, William, mark 4 in red, blue, green, brown, or gold, overglaze decorating mark, 1800s-1932.

Haviland Factory: 1886-1967

Haviland and Abbot, mark in red, overglaze importing mark, after 1886.

Haviland, Robert, mark 1 in green, underglaze factory mark, after 1924.

Haviland, Robert and Le Tanneur, mark 2 in black & red, overglaze decorating mark, 1920s-1948.

Haviland, Robert, mark 3 in red, overglaze decorating mark, after 1941.

Haviland, Robert and C. Parlon, mark 4 in black, overglaze decorating mark, after 1949.

H&C, mark 5 in green, underglaze factory mark, 1880s-1891.

Blank and Decorator Marks

HAVILAND & CIE. 1842-1931

BLANKS:

Mark A — `[HAVILAND DEPOSE]` — 1853
Incised on Tablet

Mark B — HAVILAND H&Cº — 1865
Incised

Underglaze Green Marks

Mark C — H&Cº — 1876-1879

Mark D — H&Cº — 1876-1886

Mark E — H&Cº — 1877

Mark F — H & Cº / L — 1876-1889

Mark G — H&Cº / DEPOSE — 1887

Mark H — H&Cº / L / FRANCE — 1888-1896

Mark I — Haviland / France — 1894-1931

DECORATOR MARKS:

Varied Colors Overglaze

Mark a — — prior to 1876

FABRIQUÉ PAR HAVILAND & Cº / POUR / J.W. BOTELER & BRO. / WASHINGTON

(HAVILAND & Cº LIMOGES oval mark)

Mark b — (H&C monogram mark) — 1876-1878

Mark c — HAVILAND & Cº / Limoges — 1876-1878/ 1889-1931

Mark d — HAVILAND & Cº — 1879-1883

Mark e — (H&Cº ELITE) — 1878-1883

Mark f — (H&Cº SPECIAL) — 1879-1889

Mark g — (HAVILAND LIMOGES circular mark) — 1879-1889

Mark h — Haviland / Limoget / Feu de Four — 1893-1895

Mark i — Décoré par / HAVILAND & Cº / Limoges — 1905-1930 (America) 1926-1931 (France)

HAVILAND & Co. 1875-1885

Haviland Pottery and Stoneware

Mark V — H & Cº / L — 1875-1882

Mark W — HAVILAND & Cº / Limoges — 1875-1882

Mark X — (H₃Cº) / † — 1883-1885

Mark Y — H & Cº / L HAVILAND (LIMOGES circular mark) — 1883-1885

FRANK HAVILAND 1910-1931

BLANKS:

Mark A1 — [mark] — 1910-1914

Mark A2 — [mark] — 1914-1925

Mark A3 — [mark] — 1925-1931

THEODORE HAVILAND 1892-1967

BLANKS:

Colors Usually Green Underglaze

Mark J — [mark] — 1892

Mark K — [mark] — 1892

Mark L — [mark] — 1893

Mark M — [mark] — 1894-1957

Mark N — [mark] Blue — 1912

Mark O — [mark] — 1920-1936

Mark P — [mark] — 1936-1945

Mark Q — [mark] France — 1946-1962

Mark R — [mark] France Limoges — 1962

Mark S — THEODORE HAVILAND NEW YORK — 1936
Green or Black

Mark T — [mark] Theodore Haviland New York — 1937-1956
MADE IN AMERICA
Red or Black

Mark U — [mark] HAVILAND C. H. A. — 1957
Red

DECORATOR MARKS:

Colors Green and/or Red Underglaze

Mark j — [mark] Red — probably 1892

Mark k — Porcelaine Mousseline [mark] Limoges FRANCE — 1894

Mark l — Porcelaine Mousseline [mark] Limoges FRANCE — 1894

Mark m — Porcelaine Theo. Haviland Limoges FRANCE — 1895

Mark n — [mark] Porcelaine Theo. Haviland Limoges FRANCE — 1895

Mark o — Théodore Haviland Limoges — 1897

Mark p — Théodore Haviland Limoges FRANCE — 1903

Mark q — Théodore Haviland Limoges FRANCE — 1903

Mark r — Théodore Haviland Limoges FRANCE — 1925

Mark s — [mark] HAVILAND LIMOGES FRANCE — 1958

Mark t — [mark] Haviland LIMOGES FRANCE — 1967

Frank and Theodore Haviland marks & dates. Courtesy of Haviland Collectors International Foundation.

Klingenberg, A. (AK) Charles Dwenger (AKCD) Factory: 1880s-1910

Klingenberg, A., mark 1 in red, overglaze decorating mark, early 1880s.

Klingenberg, A., mark 2 in red, overglaze decorating mark, 1880s-1890s.

Klingenberg, A., mark 3 in green, impressed or underglaze factory mark, 1880s-1890.

Klingenberg, A., mark 4 in green, underglaze factory mark, after 1891.

Klingenberg, A., mark 5 in green, underglaze factory mark, 1890s.

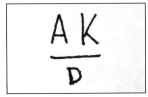

Klingenberg, A., mark 6 in green, underglaze factory mark, used after mark 5, 1890s-1910.

Klingenberg, A., mark 7 in green, underglaze factory mark, 1890s-1910.

Klingenberg, A., mark 8 in green, underglaze factory mark, 1890s-1910.

Klingenberg, A., mark 9 in red, overglaze decorating mark, 1900-1910.

Lanternier, A. Factory: 1857-Present

Lanternier, A., mark 1 in red, over-glaze decorating mark, 1890s.

Lanternier, A., mark 2 in green, underglaze factory mark, 1890s.

Lanternier, A., mark 3 in green, underglaze factory mark, 1890s.

Lanternier, A., mark 4 in green, underglaze factory mark, 1891-1914.

Lanternier, A., mark 5 in blue, overglaze export or decorating mark, before 1890.

Lanternier, A., mark 6 in red, brown, or blue, overglaze decorating mark, 1891-1914.

Lanternier, A., mark 7 in red & black, overglaze decorating mark, after WWI.

La Porcelaine Limousine (PL) Factory: 1905-1938

La Porcelaine Limousine, mark 1 in green, underglaze factory mark, 1905-1930s.

La Porcelaine Limousine, mark 2 in green, underglaze factory mark, 1905-1930s.

La Porcelaine Limousine, mark 3 in green, underglaze factory mark, 1905-1930s.

La Porcelaine Limousine, mark 4 in red, overglaze decorating mark, 1905-1930s.

Laporte, Raymonde Factory: 1883-1897

Laporte, Raymonde, mark 1 in dark green or black, underglaze factory mark, 1883-1890.

Laporte, Raymonde, mark 2 in red, overglaze decorating mark, 1891-1897.

Latrille Freres Factory: 1899-1913

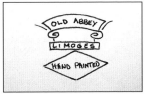

Latrille Freres, mark 1 in green, underglaze factory mark, 1899-1913.

Latrille Freres, mark 2 in red, overglaze decorating mark, 1899-1908.

Latrille Freres, mark 3 in green or red, overglaze decorating mark, 1908-1913.

Laviolette Factory: 1896-1905

Laviolette, mark in black or dark green, underglaze factory mark, 1896-1905.

Lazeyras, Rosenfeld, and Lehman Factory: 1920s

Lazeyras, Rosenfeld, and Lehman (LR&L), mark 1 in red or blue, overglaze decorating mark, 1920s.

Lazeyras, Rosenfeld, and Lehman, mark 2 in red, overglaze decorating mark, 1920s.

Lazeyras, Rosenfeld, and Lehman, mark 3 in gray or green, overglaze decorating mark, 1920s.

Lazeyras, Rosenfeld, and Lehman, mark 4 in blue, overglaze decorating mark, after 1922.

Lazeyras, Rosenfeld, and Lehman, mark 5 in blue, overglaze decorating mark, after 1922.

Legrand Factory: 1920s

Legrand, mark in green, underglaze factory mark, 1920s.

Leonard, P.H. (PHL) Factory: 1890s-1914

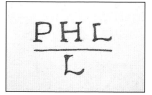

Leonard, P.H., mark 1 in red, overglaze decorating mark, 1890s-1914.

Leonard, P.H., mark 2 in red, overglaze decorating mark, 1890s-1914.

Leonard, P.H., mark 3 in red, overglaze exporting mark, 1890s-1914.

L. W. Levy & Co. (Imperial) Factory: 1880s-1920s

Levy, Imperial mark 1 in red, overglaze decorating mark, 1800s-early 1900s.

Levy, Imperial Limoges France mark 2 in red, overglaze decorating mark, 1800s-early 1900s.

Levy, L.D.C., Limoges France mark 3 in red, overglaze decorating mark, post WWI-1920s.

Limoges France Marks: 1891-1979

Limoges France, mark 1 in green, underglaze factory mark, after 1891.

Limoges France, mark 2 in green, underglaze factory mark, after 1891.

Limoges France, mark 3 in green, underglaze factory mark, after 1891.

Limoges France, mark 4 in green, underglaze factory mark, after 1891.

Limoges France, mark 5 in green, underglaze factory mark, after 1891.

Limoges France, mark 7 in green, underglaze factory mark, after 1891.

Limoges France, mark 8 in blue, overglaze decorating or exporting mark, after 1891.

Limoges France, mark in green, underglaze factory mark, 1955-1979.

Limoges France, mark 9 in gray, overglaze decorating mark, after 1908.

Limoges Castel, mark in green, gray, silver, gold, used as both underglaze factory & overglaze decorating mark, 1955-1979. Notice the words Decor MAIN (hand painted).

Martin, Charles Factory: 1880s-1935

Martin, mark 1 in green, underglaze factory mark, after 1891.

Martin, mark 2 in green, underglaze factory mark, early 1900s-1930s.

Martin, mark 3 in blue or green, overglaze decorating mark, early 1900s-mid 1930s.

Mavaleix, P.M. Factory: 1908-1914

Mc., J., D. & S. Studio: 1880s-1914

Mavaleix, mark 1 in green, underglaze factory mark, 1908-1914.

MC. D. & S., J., mark 1, overglaze decorating mark, 1880s-1890.

MC. D. & S., J., mark 2, overglaze decorating mark, 1890-1914.

Merlin, P. - Lemas (PML) Factory: 1920s

Pairpoint Studio: 1880s-1900

Merlin-Lemas, P. (PML), mark 1, underglaze factory mark, 1920s.

Merlin-Lemas, P., mark 2, overglaze decorating mark, 1920s.

Pairpoint, mark in green, overglaze decorating mark for American decorating studio, 1880s.

Paroutaud Freres Factory: 1902-1917

Pillivuyt A., Factory: 1913-1936

Paroutaud Freres, mark 1 in green, underglaze factory mark, 1903-1917.

Paroutaud Freres, mark 2 in green, underglaze factory mark, 1903-1917.

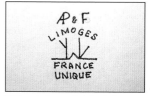

Pillivuyt, A., mark 1 in dark green, underglaze factory mark, 1920s.

Pitkin & Brooks Studio: 1872-1938

Pitkin & Brooks, mark 1 in red & green, overglaze import & decorating mark, 1872-1938.

Plainemaison Factory: 1890s-1910

Plainemaison, mark 1 in green, underglaze factory mark, 1890s-1910.

Porcelaine Pallas Studio: 1926-1950

Porcelaine Pallas, mark 1 in green, overglaze decorating mark, 1926-1950.

Pouyat, Jean (J.P.L.) Factory: 1832-1932

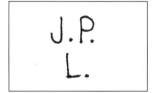

Pouyat, Jean, mark 1 in green, underglaze factory mark, 1850s-1875.

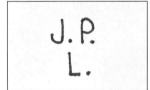

Pouyat, Jean, mark 2 in red, overglaze decorating mark, 1850s-1875.

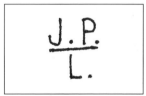

Pouyat, Jean, mark 3 in green, underglaze factory mark, after 1876-1890.

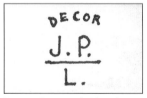

Pouyat, Jean, mark 4 in red, overglaze decorating mark, 1876-1890.

Pouyat, Jean, mark 5 in green, underglaze factory mark, 1891-1932. (Also shown Pouyat mark 8.)

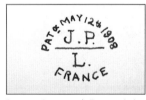

Pouyat, Jean, mark 5a, a variation of mark 5.

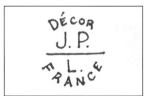

Pouyat, Jean, mark 6 in red, overglaze decorating mark, after 1890, used for a short time.

Pouyat, Jean, mark 7 in red, overglaze decorating mark, 1890s-1914.

Pouyat, Jean, mark 8 in green, overglaze decorating mark, 1914-1932.

Pouyat, Jean, mark 9, in green & pink, overglaze decorating mark, 1914-1932.

Raynaud Factory: 1920s-1930s

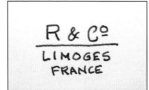

Raynaud, M. (R&Co.), mark 1, underglaze factory mark, 1920s-1930s.

Raynaud, M. (R&Co.), mark 2, overglaze decorating mark, 1920s-1930s.

Redon, Martial (MR) Factory: 1882-1896

Redon, M., mark 1 in green, underglaze factory mark, 1882-1890.

Redon, M., mark 2 in green, underglaze factory mark, 1891-1896.

Redon, M., mark 2a in green, underglaze factory mark with the word "Limoges."

Redon, M., mark 3 in red or blue, overglaze decorating mark, 1882-1896.

Redon, M., mark 4 in red, overglaze decorating mark, 1882-1896.

M. Redon, Barny & Rigoni, mark in dark green, import mark, 1902-1904.

Royal China Factory: 1900s-1920s

Royal China, mark in red, overglaze decorating mark, after 1922.

Sazerat, Leon and Blondeau (LS) Factory: 1880s-1891

Sazerat, L., mark 1 in green, underglaze factory mark, before 1891.

Sazerat, L., mark 2 in red, overglaze decorating mark, before 1891.

Sazerat, L., mark 3 in red, overglaze decorating mark, after 1891-late 1890s.

Seraput, Charles Factory: 1920s-1930s

Straus, Lewis and Sons (L.S.&S.) Factory: 1890s-1920s

Serpaut, Charles, mark in green, underglaze factory mark, 1920s-1930s.

Straus, Lewis and Sons, mark in green, blue, red, brown, or gray, overglaze export mark, 1890s-1920.

Teissonniere, Jules Factory: 1908-1940s

Teissonniere, Jules, mark 1 in black or dark green, 1908-1940s.

Teissonniere, Jules, mark 2 in black or dark green, 1908-1940s.

Texeraud, Leon Factory: 1920s

Texeraud, Leon, mark 1 in black or dark green, 1920s.

Texeraud, Leon, mark 2 in black or dark green, 1920s.

Tharaud Factory: 1920s-1960s

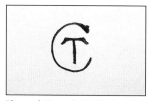

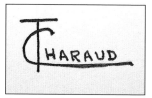

Tharaud, C., mark 1 in black or dark green, 1920s.

Tharaud, mark 2 in black or dark green, 1920s.

Touze, Lemaitre Freres & Blancher (T.L.B.) Factory: 1920s-1930s

Touze, Lemaitre Freres & Blancher, mark 1 in black or dark green, 1920s.

Touze, Lemaitre Frere, & Blancher, mark 2 in black or dark green, 1920s.

Tressemann & Vogt (T&V) Factory: 1880s-1919

Tressemann & Vogt, mark 1 in blue, overglaze export mark, 1880s-1891.

Tressemann & Vogt, mark 2 in purple, red or gold, overglaze decorating mark, early 1880s.

Tressemannn & Vogt, mark 3 in brown, overglaze decorating mark, after 1891 very rare.

Tressemann & Vogt, mark 4a in green, underglaze factory mark, early 1890s.

Tressemann & Vogt, mark 4b in green, underglaze factory mark, 1892-1907 but before mark 5a.

Tressemann & Vogt, mark 5a in green, underglaze factory mark, 1892-1907. (Also shown T&V mark 15.)

Tressemann & Vogt, mark 5b in green, underglaze factory mark. Note: This mark is found on items decorated with famous people or commemorative events.

Tressemann & Vogt, mark 6 in green, underglaze factory mark, 1892-1907 around 1900s.

Tressemann & Vogt, mark 7 in green, underglaze factory mark, 1892-1907, later part of period. (Also shown T&V mark 16b.)

Variation of Tressemann & Vogt, mark 7 in green, underglaze factory mark, 1892-1907, later part of period.

Tressemann & Vogt, mark 8 in green, underglaze factory mark, 1907-1919.

Tressemann & Vogt, mark 9 in purple, overglaze decorating mark, 1892-1907, early part of period.

Tressemann & Vogt, mark 10 in red or gold, overglaze decorating mark, 1892-1907, about 1900.

Tressemann & Vogt, mark 11 in red, brown, or gold, overglaze decorating mark, 1892-1907, later part of period.

Tressemann & Vogt, mark 12 in purple, overglaze decorating mark, 1907-1919, very rare mark.

Tressemann & Vogt, mark 13 in red, overglaze decorating mark, 1907-1919, very rare mark.

Tressemann & Vogt, mark 14 in green, overglaze decorating mark, 1907-1919, very rare mark.

Tressemann & Vogt, mark 15 in purple, overglaze decorating mark.

Tressemann & Vogt, mark 16 in purple, overglaze decorating mark, 1907-1919.

Tressemann & Vogt, mark 16b, in purple, overglaze decorating mark, like mark 16 with addition of banner with "Hand Painted," 1907-1919.

Union Ceramique (UC) Factory: 1901-1938

Union Ceramique, mark 1 in green, underglaze factory mark, 1909-1938.

Union Ceramique, mark 2 in red, overglaze decorating mark, 1909-1938. (Also shown mark 1 above & import mark below.)

Union Ceramique, mark 3 in green, underglaze factory mark, 1909-1938.

Union Limousine Factory: 1908-Present

V.F. Factory: 1890s

Union Limousine, mark 1 in green, underglaze factory mark, 1930s-1950s.

V.F., mark 1 in green, underglaze factory mark, early 1890s.

Vignaud Freres Factory: 1911-1970

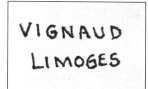

Vignaud Freres, mark 1 in green, underglaze factory mark, after 1911-1938.

Vignaud Freres, mark 2 in green, overglaze decorating mark, 1911-1938.

Vignaud Freres, mark 3 in green, underglaze factory mark, 1938 and after.

Vultury Freres Factory: 1887-1904

Wanamaker's Studio: 1900s

Vultury Freres, mark 1 in green, underglaze factory mark, 1887-1904.

Wanamaker's, mark in green, over-glaze import mark, early 1900s.

Current Reproduction Marks

Reproduction mark, gold, black, blue, red, crown w/crossed swords.

Reproduction mark, gold, black, blue, red, fleur-de-lis above "Limoges China."

Reproduction mark, gold, black, blue, red, variation of the fleur-de-lis above "Limoges China."

Reproduction mark, gold, black, blue, red, variation of the fleur-de-lis above "Limoges China."

Reproduction mark, ROC.

Reproduction mark, ROC above "Limoges China."

Reproduction mark, L.F. Fine Porcelain Limoges P.R.C. or R.O.C.

Bibliography

Albis, Jean d', and Celeste Romanet. *La Porcelaine de Limoges.* Paris: Sous le Vent, 1980.

Allon, Janet. *The Business of Bliss, How to Profit from Doing What You Love.* New York: Hearst Books, 1999.

Cameron, Elisabeth. *Encyclopedia of Pottery and Porcelain: 1800-1960.* New York: Facts on File Publications, 1986.

Celebrating 150 Years of Haviland China: 1842-1992. Haviland Collectors Internationale Foundation, 1992.

Chefetz, Sheila. *Antiques for the Table.* New York: Penguin Books USA, Inc., 1993.

DuBay, Debby. *Living With Limoges.* Atglen, Pennsylvania: Schiffer Publishing, Ltd., 2001.

———. *Antique Limoges at Home.* Atglen, Pennsylvania: Schiffer Publishing, Ltd., 2002.

———. *Collecting Hand Painted Limoges Porcelain - Boxes to Vases.* Atglen, Pennsylvania: Schiffer Publishing, Ltd., 2004.

Gaston, Mary Frank. *The Collector's Encyclopedia of Limoges Porcelain,* Second Edition. Paducah, Kentucky: Collector Books, 1994.

———. *The Collector's Encyclopedia of Limoges Porcelain,* Third Edition. Paducah, Kentucky: Collector Books, 2000.

Hynes, Angela. *The Pleasures of Afternoon Tea.* Los Angeles: HP Books, 1987.

Israel, Andrea. *Taking Tea.* New York, New York: Michael Friedman Publishing Group, Inc. 1988.

Jaffe, Deborah. *Victoria.* London, Carlton Books Limited, 2000.

Kamm, Dorothy. *Antique Trader's Comprehensive Guide to American Painted Porcelain.* Norfolk, Virginia: Antique Trader Books, 2000.

———. *American Painted Porcelain: Collector's Identification and Value Guide.* Paducah, Kentucky: Collector Books, 1997, values updated 1999.

———. *American Painted Porcelain Jewelry: Miniature Masterpieces.* Antiques & Collecting Magazine. Illinois, Lightner Publishing Corporation, April 2000.

King, M. Dalton. *Special Teas.* Philadelphia, Pennsylvania: A Running Press/Kenan Book, 1992.

Kovel, Ralph M., and Terry H. Kovel. *Dictionary of Marks: Pottery and Porcelain.* New York: Crown Publishers, Inc., 1953 and 1972.

———. *Kovels' New Dictionary of Marks.* New York: Crown Publishers, Inc., 1986.

Lehner, Lois. *Lehner's Encyclopedia of U.S. Marks on Pottery, Porcelain & Clay.* Paducah, Kentucky: Collector Books, 1988.

Limoges, Raymonde. *American Limoges.* Paducah, Kentucky: Collector Books, 1996.

Manchester, Carole. *French Tea, The Pleasures of the Table.* New York: Hearst Books, 1993.

Phillips, Phoebe. *The Collectors' Encyclopedia of Antiques.* London, England: Crown Publishing, 1978.

Revi, Albert Christian. *The Spinning Wheel's Complete Book of Antiques.* New York: Grosset & Dunlap, 1977.

Reed, Alan B. *Encyclopedia of Picard China.* Paducah, Kentucky: Collector Books, 1995.

Sandon, Henry. *Coffee Pots and Tea Pots for the Collector.* New York: Arco Publishing Co., Inc., 1974.

Stewart, Martha. *Living.* December 1994, January 1995.

Strumph, Faye. *Limoges Boxes, A Complete Guide.* Iola, Wisconsin: Krause Publications, 2000.

Travis, Nora. *Haviland China: The Age of Elegance.* Atglen, Pennsylvania: Schiffer Publishing, Ltd., 1997.

Waterbrook-Clyde, Keith, and Thomas Waterbrook-Clyde. *The Decorative Art of Limoges Porcelain and Boxes.* Atglen, Pennsylvania: Schiffer Publishing, Ltd., 1999.

Wynter, Harriet. *An Introduction to European Porcelain.* New York: Thomas Y. Crowell Company, 1972.

Index by Maker

Add to Your Pottery and Porcelain Reference Library

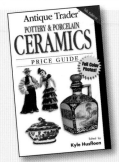
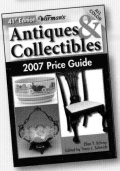